Sociology of
Religion

John Barter

**Advanced
TopicMaster**

Series editor
Jill Swale

Acknowledgements: thank you to Bill Bayton for a wonderful introduction to sociology, and to David Martin and Eileen Barker for developing my interest in the sociology of religion. Love and thanks go to my family: to Janet, for her editing and research skills, her patience and support; to Joe, for his technical support; to Becky, for her cuddles; and to my parents for giving me the best possible start in life. Finally, thanks to Tina for the hours of word processing and to the students of Wrenn School who were guinea pigs for much of this material.

Philip Allan Updates
Market Place
Deddington
Oxfordshire
OX15 0SE

Orders
Bookpoint Ltd, 130 Milton Park, Abingdon, Oxfordshire, OX14 4SB
tel: 01235 827720
fax: 01235 400454
e-mail: uk.orders@bookpoint.co.uk
Lines are open 9.00 a.m.–5.00 p.m., Monday to Saturday, with a 24-hour message answering service. You can also order through the Philip Allan Updates website: www.philipallan.co.uk

© Philip Allan Updates 2007

ISBN 978-1-84489-700-1

Printed in Spain

Philip Allan Updates' policy is to use papers that are natural, renewable and recyclable products and made from wood grown in sustainable forests. The logging and manufacturing processes are expected to conform to the environmental regulations of the country of origin.

Contents

Introduction

Unless you practise a particular religion and attend a place of worship regularly, you may take the view that religion is irrelevant. However, on reflection, it is the case that religion has had a key influence on societies, both past and present. Some of the most famous buildings in the world were built to celebrate God and to bring people together in worship. Wars have been fought in the name of one God or another. Millions of Jews were killed in the Second World War and also in other periods of history. Terrorist acts, such as suicide bombings, are sometimes carried out in the name of God. Some contemporary acts, for example vegetarianism, yoga and meditation, stem from eastern religious traditions. You may have a faith school in your area and there will almost certainly be different places of worship. You will have seen art, plays or television programmes with religious content. You may feel that this has had little impact on your life, but there is no doubt that religion does have an impact on the behaviour of people.

There are claims that society is undergoing secularisation (i.e. religion is becoming less important and influential). Is that a good or a bad thing? It may mean that in the future you will no longer be inconvenienced by people knocking on your door to tell you about God and that *Songs of Praise* will no longer interfere with your Sunday television viewing, but on what would the morals of people be based? There is an argument that our society is more crime-ridden than in the past because religion is a less powerful influence in the socialisation of children. If this argument is true, you could become a victim of crime, so a lack of religion may impact on your life in that way.

This book will not try to convert you to any religion. However, it does aim to show you that religion is a fascinating area of social behaviour. You don't have to be religious to study it. In fact, it may be an advantage if you are not because you may be more open minded. Whether or not you have a faith, you should be able to find much that will interest you.

The book follows the key examination specifications. Its primary focus is on the UK, but it also draws links to global phenomena, as Britain's religious and social life is heavily influenced by religion across the world. The book contains hints on how to expand your knowledge and tasks to help you develop analytical skills. The chapters can be treated as stand-alone sections and covered in any order. However, you should be able to make connections between them, particularly in terms of secularisation. Chapters 5 and 6, for example, contain much evidence that you could use to support the theories outlined in Chapter 4. At the end of each chapter, there are references to websites and further reading to develop your interest in specific areas. You could also follow up one or more of the research suggestions, either formally for coursework or as an extended project, or informally to satisfy your intellectual curiosity. There is a glossary of key words and definitions at the end of the book, which you should try to learn.

I hope that you enjoy the book. Good luck with your studies!

John Barter

How religion is defined

Why do definitions matter?

If people in the street were asked what 'religion' means, most would be sure that they knew. However, if pushed to explain the idea in their heads, they might find it difficult. How one person defines 'religion' may differ radically from the definition provided by someone else. In everyday life (and on most topics) this would not matter too much, because as long as we have a rough comprehension of a term, we can understand what other people mean when they use the term. However, most people tend to avoid talking about religion because of conflicting views about the subject.

Sociologists do not avoid talking about matters that could cause differences in opinion with their peers. In fact, some sociologists enjoy the subject *because* it challenges them to think more deeply about topics. However, when sociologists discuss topics such as religion, they cannot risk the ambiguity that we might accept from people in everyday life. They have to be sure that other sociologists will understand exactly what they mean. Sociologists do more than talk — they research. This research involves collecting data or evidence to support, or to challenge, an argument or theory. To do this they must operationalise their concepts, i.e. define them in such a way that they can be measured effectively. Therefore, it is important that sociologists of religion define the term 'religion' in order to be clear what it is they will be measuring. They can then make their points effectively and, as a result, other sociologists can check the reliability of their data and the resulting theory.

Task 1.1

(a) Think about the word 'religion'. Make a list of all the things that you associate with it.

(b) Use the points on your list to develop your own definition of religion. Ideally, it should consist of one sentence.

How do sociologists define religion?

The chances are that your answer to Task 1.1 will have been influenced by your own experience of religion. This experience might have been gained at school, from participating in a specific kind of organised religion or from something you have witnessed through the media. It may refer to the major world religions — to religious figures, holy books, places of worship and the like. Some sociologists have used this approach. As a result, they have developed a substantive (exclusive/narrow) definition of religion. Others have criticised this approach for being ethnocentric. Their argument is that a substantive definition is too heavily influenced by personal culture and experience. Such an approach excludes beliefs and practices that fall outside the mainstream experience of religion.

Critics of the substantive approach to religion advocate a functional (inclusive/broad) definition of religion that includes any set of beliefs and practices that guides the lives of its followers. A functional definition includes everything covered by the substantive definition together with a wider range of other features. The major criticism of this approach is that it is too broad to be of sociological value.

By the end of this chapter you should understand both positions and be able to say which approach you feel is most useful in analysing what counts as 'religion'.

Functional definitions of religion

A substantive approach to defining religion is most likely to only view pictures a, b, c and h in Task 1.2 as religious symbols. This is because they relate to something that is instantly recognisable as religious. However, a functional definition would allow any of the pictures to be indicative of religion. Why?

A functional definition of religion looks beyond the apparent 'religious' value of a symbol and asks what it does for the adherents or followers. To be religious, it should guide their lives. To do so, the functionalist sociologist Emile Durkheim (1858–1917) believed it would have a sacred quality. He argued that all known religious beliefs have:

> …one common characteristic…division of the world into two domains, one containing all that is sacred, the other all that is profane. But by sacred things one must not understand simply those personal beings which are called Gods or spirits; a rock, a tree, a spring, a pebble, a piece of wood, a house, in a word anything can be sacred.
>
> E. Durkheim, *The Elementary Forms of Religious life* (1982)
> (first published in French, 1912)

Task 1.2

(a) 'Ichthys' (Christian fish)

(b) Sikh Khalsa sign

ArkReligion.com/Alamy

(c) A statue of Buddha

TopFoto

(d) A baobab tree

Paul L.H.Cook (http://langabi.name)

(e) Rocks

(f) A Communist sign

MalcolmFairman/Alamy

(g) A US flag

TopFoto

(h) The Koran

TopFoto

Consider the above images. Which ones represent something religious? Give reasons for your answer.

Guidance

You might wish to consider the points made on page 6 on definitions of religion.

By 'sacred', Durkheim meant that adherents were in awe of it. The sacred was deemed to have a powerful quality and, therefore, would 'prescribe how a man should comfort himself', whereas the profane was ordinary and of little value. It would not influence a person's behaviour. Importantly, the sacred value was recognised by a group, not just by an individual. Their common belief united them in consensus. As a result, Durkheim defined religion in the following way:

> A religion is a unified system of beliefs and practices relative to sacred things, that is to say, set apart and forbidden — beliefs and practices which unite into one single moral community called a church, all those who adhere to them.
>
> E. Durkheim, 1912

The sacred is easy to see in the major religions of the world. In Christianity, bread, wine and water take on a sacred quality when 'blessed'. In Hinduism, cows are regarded as sacred, but goats are not. In Islam, the Koran (considered to be the word of God) is seen to be sacred and should not touch the ground. It follows that objects being designated as 'sacred' leads adherents to treat them in a reverential way. The sacred quality is bound up in notions of higher powers that adherents gain from 'holy' texts or stories. It means that adherents are drawn together because they have beliefs in common. These beliefs are reinforced by group activity. In mainstream religion, this is seen as involving 'worship'.

The functionalist definition of religion allows common beliefs and practices other than world religions to be seen as 'religion'. Robertson (1970), writing at a time when a significant part of the world was under communist rule or influenced by communist ideas, argued that the functional (inclusive) definition allowed communism to be seen as 'religion'. This was because communism strongly influenced the lives of followers and demanded a strong commitment to certain kinds of behaviour. Followers were willing to do this because they valued the arguments initially presented by Marx; these could be interpreted as having a sacred quality in the same way that the holy books of the major world religions do. Robertson went on to argue that, in functional terms, it was not just communism that could be considered as a religion: 'not only political ideologies such as nationalism and fascism, but also other belief systems such as secularism, humanism, psychoanalysis "as a way of life" and so on'.

Your answer to Task 1.3 might cover interests such as vegetarianism, football and music cultures. Vegetarianism, although employed by major world religions such as Buddhism, also influences the lives of people who would not consider themselves to be religious, in a commonsense understanding of the term. From a functional perspective, animals would be seen as 'sacred'. This reverence towards animals often influences the wider behaviour of adherents and links them to others, although not necessarily in regular meetings. For

Task 1.3

Are there other collective interests that strongly influence or guide the lives of people you know, but that would not be considered religious in substantive terms?

Guidance

These collective interests would need to affect the behaviour of followers in order to be considered influential. 'Sacred' objects or beliefs would be created. Followers would be drawn together with other like-minded people.

example, vegetarians are likely to care about the wider environment, not just animals. This could include care for other members of the community, recycling, pacifism and ethical consumerism.

Football could be considered to inspire religious fervour. Supporters unite together, regularly attend their favourite team's stadium (a church?), sing songs that praise their teams (hymns?), tell and write stories about past heroes and suffering ('holy' stories), and wear outfits — shirts in particular — that are seen to have a 'sacred' quality. Supporters live their lives around the football calendar in much the same way as Christians do around the Christian calendar.

Music cultures, too, could be viewed in a similar way, having a direct and long-lasting effect on the lives of followers. The song *God is a DJ* by Faithless provides a good example of this argument.

Box 1.1
Faithless

- A review of one of their concerts finished with the following:

  Live on stage is Faithless, their arena, their church, their Mecca…It's good to see dance religion breathing loud and clear.

- A fan's website offered the following observations:

  I think Faithless are fascinating because they seem to manage to combine a deep message with real celebration…Maxi Jazz is a unique front man — he comes across with real authority and spirituality, there is nothing quite like several thousand people leaping up and down being led by him singing 'this is our church, this is where we heal our hurts'…

- Another wrote of Maxi Jazz:

  He manages to be a 'small c' charismatic and reminds me of a prophet figure. Faithless did make me walk back out into the multicultural night of central Birmingham with a new freshness about inclusivity. Not many preachers do that.

  Source: http://jonnybaker.blogs.com/jonnybaker/2005/11/faithless_at_br.html

Task 1.4

Find the music and lyrics to *God is a DJ* by Faithless. What are the messages in the lyrics? What images are created by the music?

Maxi Jazz, the singer and lyric writer of *God is a DJ*, uses a play on words when he talks about 'God'. By 'God' he means himself; not God as in the Almighty, but G.O.D. as in the 'Grand Oral Disseminator' (i.e. the MC). The implication is that the MC can come to be seen as a god by his followers. The music venue can be seen as a church; it takes people out of their ordinary existence and gives them something more. It is a place where followers heal their psychological hurt, through togetherness, through attendance and in uniting around the message. The notion of a religious or spiritual quality has not escaped those who see and hear Faithless.

Task 1.5

How persuasive are the arguments that vegetarianism, supporting football and music cultures can be religious? Compare your answers to this task with the evaluations by sociologists that follow.

Evaluation of the functional approach

Strengths

The functional definition of religion goes beyond notions that religion equates to Christianity or one of the other major faiths. This allows us to consider more strongly the impact on behaviour, which is the essence of sociology. It also helps sociologists to avoid ethnocentricity. However, Bruce (1995) sees this as a major disadvantage, because sociologists using this approach talk about something that is unrecognisable to others.

Weaknesses

- The functional definition does not allow for the fact that people may attend perhaps because it is considered 'the right thing to do', but not believe (Budd 1970). For example, new immigrant communities often appear to be strongly religious in order to maintain their collective identity. This may be only for the sake of appearances.
- Neither does it allow for the fact that some people may believe themselves to be religious, but choose not to meet with others as a 'moral community',

instead remaining happily privatised and living their ideals in the way they conduct themselves. According to Davie (1994), an increasing number of people believe without belonging to a particular religious community.

- Functional definitions are biased towards the view that we need a moral or values system to guide our lives or we would, as individuals and a society, crumble. However, some get on with their lives without thinking deeply about it and manage to 'survive' psychologically without religion (Worsley 1968).
- Sacredness is a subjective and relative notion. It cannot be accurately measured. What one person sees as sacred in one context may not be so to another. Some values are referred to as sacred (e.g. 'democracy'), but this may not give them a religious quality. Robertson argues that people using a functional definition are often contradictory in their own work, using functional definitions when talking about religion in general terms, but using substantive definitions when providing concrete examples.

Substantive definitions of religion

As a result of the criticisms of the functional (inclusive/broad) definition of religion, some sociologists prefer to use the substantive (exclusive/narrow) definition. Such a definition excludes all those beliefs and practices that are not obviously religious. The key focus of substantive definitions is on belief in, and worship of, a higher being or beings more powerful than humanity; we usually understand these to be a God or gods. However, Giddens (1993) has argued that 'people may believe in and revere a "divine force" rather than personalised Gods'.

For some religions, for example Buddhism and the Church of Scientology, this 'divine force' is to be found within the individual. Therefore, religion could, in a substantive sense, be experience of the Holy.

Robertson (1970) used the following substantive definition: 'Religious culture is that set of beliefs and symbols (and values deriving directly therefrom)

Task 1.6

Given that much sociological theory and research reflects a substantive viewpoint, you should improve your basic knowledge of the major world religions, particularly Christianity and Islam. For most, this will involve revisiting work covered earlier in school; your revision need only be on a basic level.

Copy out Table 1.1. Use a Key Stage 3 religious studies book or the website www.bbc.co.uk/religion to help you fill it in. The process of completing the table will reinforce the basic elements of the substantive definition of religion.

Table 1.1 Summary of the characteristics of the major world religions

Characteristic	Christianity	Islam	Hinduism	Buddhism	Sikhism	Judaism
God						
Holy figure						
Holy books						
Place of worship						
Religious leaders						
Local leaders						
Key rules						
What happens when you die?						
Festivals						
Sacred places						
Symbols						
Special clothing						

pertaining to a distinction between an empirical and a **super-empirical, transcendent** reality; the affairs of the empirical being subordinated to the non-empirical'. As a result, belief systems such as communism, nationalism and vegetarianism are seen as religious 'equivalents' or 'surrogates', because they have qualities of a religion but do not have a belief in a higher being. From this point of view, they are not religions.

Evaluation of the substantive approach

Strengths

- The substantive definition of religion meets the views of people in everyday life and of **theologians**. It makes sociology accessible and understandable to non-sociologists (Budd 1970).

- Bruce argues a similar point when he writes that he prefers the substantive definition because:

> …this allows me to formulate a number of theories which I believe have considerable explanatory scope. Religion, then, consists of beliefs, actions, and institutions which assume the existence of supernatural entities with powers of action, or impersonal powers or processes possessed of moral purpose. Such a formulation seems to encompass what ordinary people mean when they talk of religion.
>
> Bruce, *Religion in the Modern World: from Cathedrals to Cults* (1996)

Weaknesses

- Beliefs in God or divine forces are notoriously hard to define. Budd (1970) argues that 'people are reluctant to answer questions, especially if they are neither orthodox believers nor self-consciously secularist…perhaps because it is hard for them to make their beliefs explicit'. Their 'beliefs may bear little relationship to official ones' and are sometimes contradictory.
- Limiting definitions of religion to substantive notions risks ethnocentric conclusions and may fail to explain accurately beliefs and practices that have a religious quality. Evans-Pritchard (1956), an anthropologist, studied an east African tribe called the Nuer. He found that their references to God, not as a noun but through adjectives, verbs or metaphors, did not relate to western understandings of God and were, initially, confusing. It could lead us to miss important things or to be 'unduly "charitable" to beliefs by interpreting them as sensible interpretations of reality rather than as false or crazy' (Budd 1970).
- Robertson (1970) agrees with the above point, arguing that too many concepts employed in the sociology of religion are derived from Christianity.

Note: You will find that, although Robertson has tried to avoid this trap, much of the sociology referenced in this book relates to the Christian world because this has been the subject of most of the writing about the UK and the developed world.

Summary

- Accurate measurement of religious processes, are, ideally, based upon agreed definitions of religion. However, this is rarely possible in any area of sociology because definitions reflect competing perspectives on social life.
- Some sociologists argue that definitions of religion should aim to avoid ethnocentricity; they should not be based upon our own cultural expectations if we are to avoid missing important components of religion.

Task 1.7

Assess how a definition of religion impacts on the research evidence selected for study by a sociologist of religion.

Guidance

This is structured like a typical AQA question and, therefore, requires a range of skills. You need to:

- show breadth of knowledge and understanding by referring to the two main definitions of religion and the arguments for them
- examine the strengths and weaknesses of both definitions and show how a definition of religion impacts on the research evidence selected — you could refer to the arguments of Robertson, Bruce and Davie
- plan the whole essay before you begin writing to enable you to interweave knowledge and evaluation points throughout your answer

First, explain the two main definitions of religion — functional and substantive. Give examples of 'religions' that come under the banner of each definition to indicate how the research evidence chosen might be affected. For example, a sociologist using a substantive definition might look at the use of songs and chants in a church or temple in creating a 'religious' experience. However, a sociologist using a functional definition may compare these with those employed by a football crowd or a concert audience.

The evaluative element of the essay should consider the strengths and weaknesses of each approach. For example, the substantive approach lays itself open to the criticism of ethnocentricity, but would produce research that ordinary people might recognise as religious. The functional definition should reduce the possibility of ethnocentricity, but could produce evidence that is too generalised to be of worth to the general population; such sociologists then run the risk of being seen as 'living in ivory towers' and of being out of touch with the real world. Should sociology respond to commonsense notions or should it challenge them?

The essay should conclude with a summing up of your assessment of the strengths and weaknesses of each definitional approach. Which do you think offers the way forward? Try not to sit on the fence and say you can see the merits of both; opt for one or the other. This, if justified properly with good reasons, would earn more marks for evaluation.

- There are two main definitions of religion, functional and substantive:
  - A functional definition is based on how the 'religion' draws people together and how it guides their lives. It includes those institutions that people ordinarily see as religions (e.g. Christianity and Islam); it could also include

other practices that guide people's lives, such as football or a music genre. This is why it is sometimes called a broad definition.

– A substantive definition excludes those practices not ordinarily seen as religious. This is why it is called a 'narrow' or 'exclusive' definition. It focuses on institutions and organisations that people see as religious (or which claim to be religious).

Research suggestions

- Can following a football team be considered religious? You could interview football followers about the level of impact the sport has on their lives, the meanings of the songs they sing, their favourite players, the club symbols etc. Does the functional definition stand up to scrutiny?
- What does it mean to be religious? You could gain answers from followers of substantive religions such as Christianity, Islam and Hinduism. This would help to develop an ideal substantive definition of religion.

Useful websites

- www.cod.edu/PEOPLE/FACULTY/raepple/ElecExcs/Chap2Ex.htm
  This page is a 'test-yourself' exercise regarding the usefulness of a range of definitions of religion and provides answers so that you can get immediate feedback on your opinions.
- www.sociology.org.uk/reldefc.doc
  Sociology.org is an excellent site worth visiting for a range of topics. This page is a detailed set of revision notes on the definition of religion.
- http://atheism.about.com/od/religiondefinition/a/types.htm
  This site introduces the reader to the divisions between functional and substantive definitions of religion. Its atheistic focus is worth following up using the links to other areas on the site.

Further reading

- Aldridge, A. (2000) *Religion in the Contemporary World*, Polity.
  Chapter 2 is a detailed consideration of the most appropriate definition to use in the sociological study of religion.
- Bruce, S. (1995) *Religion in Modern Britain*, Oxford.
  The preface carries a short and accessible argument for the use of the substantive definition.

The functions of religion

What is meant by functions?

This is a core area of the sociology of religion. The basic issue under question is the role of religion in society and for the members of society:

- Why does religion exist?
- What 'jobs' does it do?

There is a general (but not total) acceptance that religion is universal; it is found in all societies and in all historical periods. There is increasing concern, however, that religion as we know it (usually via a substantive definition) is dying. Will something else — perhaps those practices considered under the broader functional definition — take its place? If not, what will guide people's lives and from where will their morals be derived?

There are two main approaches to explaining the functions of religion:

- The **macro** or structural approach examines the impact that religion has on the whole society and, therefore, on the behaviour of individual members. There are three main structural approaches: functionalism, Marxism and feminism.
- The **micro** approach focuses on the functions that religions perform for individual adherents (and the impact that these in combination have on society). It is developed with reference to the work of the phenomenologists Peter Berger and Thomas Luckmann, who built on the theoretical foundation provided by Max Weber.

The emphasis in this chapter is on classical theorists, because these provide a firm foundation for further study. Some contemporary sociologists relate their arguments to this work. Fenn (2001) notes that: 'Whether for positive or negative reasons, then the seminal works of Marx, Weber [and] Durkheim… continue to provide the basis for contemporary discussions, arguments and discoveries in the sociology of religion'.

Functionalists on the functions of religion

Functionalists, in general, see society operating as a consensual whole. It is organised by its structures or institutions, which work interdependently to create a consensus. The individual members submit to the collective will. As an agent of secondary socialisation, religion functions to maintain this system. Essentially, functionalists argue that religion provides society with consensus by acting as:

- a means of uniting people by bringing them together in ritual and celebration, for example, the Jesus Army
- a moral system providing the norms and values that guide the behaviour patterns of individual members
- a means of explaining the inexplicable and, therefore, avoiding stress that could disrupt individual lives and the smooth running of society

Emile Durkheim was the pioneer of the functionalist perspective. He developed a functional definition of religion, arguing that religions designate some elements of society as sacred. This draws adherents together as a community (or 'church') to worship 'the sacred' through appropriate rituals. This enables the society or group to develop a collective consciousness — a shared way of thinking, based on sharing the same norms and values. It also helps develop social solidarity — a feeling of togetherness that makes the group and its individual members feel psychologically stronger.

Members of the Jesus Army use song to bring them together

Task 2.1

Consider the role of Christian churches in drawing people into a collective group. The first of the extracts below is from a novel about life in South Africa and the other is from an oral history of life in the Welsh valleys.

How do these extracts illustrate the role that religion can play in creating social solidarity and a collective consciousness?

Extract 1

There is a lamp outside the church, the lamp they light for the services. There are women of the church sitting on the red earth under the lamp; they are dressed in white dresses, each with a green cloth about her neck. They rise when the party approaches, and one breaks into a hymn, with a high note that cannot be sustained; but others come in underneath it, and support and sustain it, and some men come in too, with the deep notes and the true. Kumalo takes off his hat and he and his wife and his friend join in also, while the girl stands and watches in wonder. It is a hymn of thanksgiving, and man remembers God in it, and prostrates himself and gives thanks for the Everlasting Mercy. And it echoes in the bare red hills and over the bare red fields of the broken tribe. And it is sung in love and humility and gratitude, and the humble simple people pour their lives into the song.

Source: A. Paton, *Cry, The Beloved Country* (1972)

Extract 2

All our social life was all with the chapel. Because there was something there every night of the week for us. Either little plays, or there'd be children's operettas. Or the big choir then, we'd have the cantatas. And there'd be Young People's Society and Cwrdd Gweddi as we'd call it. Prayer meeting was on a Monday night. And then there was Gyfeillach as we used to call it on Thursday night. Oh, it used to be years ago, we were over 300 members in this little church here. In our chapel. Even the gallery and all used to be full there. Everybody went to chapel then. That was our way of life. Our social life was all around the church. And it wasn't dull, mind. We had an awful lot of fun.

Source: B. Jones and B. Thomas, *Coal's Domain* (1993)

Durkheim's views (1912) developed from his study of totemism in Australia. This religion designated a specific object such as a rock or tree as sacred — 'the flag of the clan'. The clan 'is essentially a group of individuals who share the same name and rally around the same sign'. He justified his focus on totemism by saying that it is 'the most primitive and simple religion which it is possible to find…as close as possible to the origins of evolution'. By studying such a basic form of religion, he argued that its essential elements became clearer. These could then be generalised to modern society, which was more complex in its organisation. His study suggested that the main function of religion was 'to rouse man above himself and to make him lead a life superior to that which he would lead if he followed only his spontaneous desires: beliefs express this life in *representations*; rites organise it and regulate its functioning'.

In Durkheim's view, in worshipping a god, the clan or social group were worshipping a collective identity. This function would be common and indispensable to all societies and explained why religion was universal. The religion (and the totem) was a symbolic representation of the community. It followed, therefore, that religion did not need a god because that was not the point of religion; this is why Durkheim preferred a functional rather than a substantive definition of religion. He argued that there was no functional difference between religions that worshipped a god and religions that worshipped sacred things such as rocks, trees or flags:

> What essential difference is there between an assembly of Christians celebrating the principal dates of the life of Christ, or of Jews remembering the exodus from Egypt and a reunion of citizens commemorating the promulgation of a new moral or legal system or some great event of national life?
>
> E. Durkheim, 1912

Task 2.2

Think back to the research you did on the major world religions from a substantive viewpoint for Task 1.6.

(a) Is it possible to identify:
  - beliefs that may express to adherents the purpose of their lives? Give examples.
  - rites or rituals that organise and regulate an adherent's life? Give examples.

(b) How might these prevent adherents following their 'spontaneous desires'?

(c) If adherents were prevented from following 'spontaneous desires', what would be the potential benefits for them and their society? Do you share Durkheim's view that this would be a positive thing? Give reasons for your answer.

Durkheim also argued that totemism acted as a kind of 'mythological sociology' in that it helped adherents to understand their social world. Sciences, such as psychology, could do this to some extent in the modern world. However, Durkheim argued that sciences do not draw people together in the same way that religion does, so religion would still be necessary. Science could explain the profane world; religion would explain the sacred one.

Civil religion

Durkheim's question in the quotation on page 19 was taken up by neo-Durkheimians such as Bellah (1967), who coined the term civil religion to explain how nation states can act collectively to create social solidarity and a collective consciousness. In the USA, nationwide rituals (such as those related to the inauguration of a president or annually on 4 July and Thanksgiving) unite people above geographical, ethnic, or (substantive) religious membership. Bellah argued that like any substantive religion, civil religion in the USA has its own symbols:

- **Sacred texts** — the Declaration of Independence and the Gettysburg address
- **Sacred heroes** — past presidents, for example Lincoln and Washington
- **Sacred places** — Lincoln Memorial, the White House
- **Sacred historical events** — War of Independence

Task 2.3

If we were to apply the same principle of civil religion to the UK, what would be its sacred texts, heroes, places and events?

In terms of the UK, a classic study by Shills and Young (1953) examined the effects of the coronation of Queen Elizabeth II in 1953. Your parents may well recall the community spirit that developed during her 1977 jubilee, when many street parties were held. You might have been included in a street party to celebrate the new Millennium. If so, can you remember how people interacted with each other and how you felt?

Finally, you might consider how each national community within the UK pulls together at times of important sporting events such as the World Cup; people talk about matches to strangers, with animation and pride. They may 'fly the flag' to show their commitment to the 'sacred heroes'.

Can you remember what it was like during the last football World Cup?

Evaluation of functionalist interpretations

Strengths

- Malinowski (1884–1942) supported the Durkheimian account with his study of the pre-industrial society of the Trobriand Islanders (in the Pacific Ocean). He found that religious ritual was applied to stressful situations, such as fishing trips and the inexact practice of growing food to feed the whole community. This supports Durkheim's notion that religion creates social solidarity and explains events that are beyond the understanding of the community.
- Parsons (1902–79) argued that religion plays a key role in 'pattern maintenance' in society; in other words, ensuring social order or stability. It does this by creating rules, norms and patterns that guide the behaviour of individuals and reduce the potential of the selfish ego to produce anti-social behaviour. This supports Durkheim's argument that religion provides a moral system and enables social life to take place.
- Lukes (1981) offered a detailed appraisal of Durkheim's work. He argued that: 'Despite the many criticisms that have been justifiably advanced against this work…it remains a major and profound contribution to the sociology of religion.' Giddens (1993) agrees, arguing that Durkheim's work is 'the single most influential study in the sociology of religion'.

Limitations

- The structural determinism of functionalists like Durkheim is open to criticism. Where Durkheim suggests that without organised religion individuals will be selfish, phenomenologists suggest that people can be individually moral and religious, following their own designated ethical paths. These themes are taken up later in the chapter.
- Conflict theorists such as Marxists and feminists criticise the lack of a 'dark side' to functionalist analyses of religion for individuals and society. 'The part religion can play in stimulating social conflict and legitimising inequality and oppression is ignored' (Aldridge 2000). This theme is taken up in the following two sections of this chapter.
- Durkheim's methodology has also been much criticised. His arguments were based on secondary evidence compiled by a range of individuals such as missionaries, who were rather ethnocentric and lacked methodological rigour. Lukes (1981) argues that his choice of totemism was unrepresentative; it was 'highly atypical and specialised even within Australia' and that 'there is no evidence at all that Australian totemism is the earliest form of totemism (let alone religion)'. Aldridge (2000) suggests that Durkheim was overly subjective, making the facts fit his hypothesis rather than vice versa.

Marxists on the functions of religion

Marx (1818–83) wrote relatively little on religion and its functions. However, what he did write has been extremely influential. It supports his conflict theory of social-class differences in society. Marx adopted what he called historical materialism to describe the past, present and future of human relationships; he argued that this was based on observations of events in the *real* world. Apart from primitive societies, which Marx argued had been based on equality, he felt that all other societies had been built upon unequal relationships, with a small minority (the ruling class) using economic power to exploit the majority (the working class). In capitalist societies, he called the ruling class the 'bourgeoisie' and the working class the 'proletariat'. The economic relations between the two classes were called infrastructure or 'the base'. On top was the superstructure — the institutions of society that supported the maintenance of the infrastructure and the common interests of the ruling class. One element of the superstructure was seen to be religion; others were institutions such as education and the mass media.

The key function of religion for Marx is the creation of false class-consciousness. This is a condition in the minds of working-class people that their position at the bottom of society is fair and appropriate. As a result, they do not feel

Task 2.4

Read the following extracts from the New Testament. How would Marx have used them to support his view that religion was used to make the working class accept their position?

Extract 1

Refrain from anger and turn from wrath; do not fret — it leads only to evil. For evil men will be cut off, but those who hope in the Lord will inherit the land…Better the little that the righteous have than the wealth of many wicked; for the power of the wicked will be broken but the Lord upholds the righteous…

Psalm 37, *New Testament and Psalms*

Extract 2

Then Jesus said to his disciples, 'I tell you the truth, it is hard for a rich man to enter the kingdom of heaven. Again, I tell you it is easier for a camel to go through the eye of a needle than for a rich man to enter the kingdom of God.'

Matthew 19:23–24, *New Testament and Psalms*

exploited and, therefore, do not rise up against the ruling class. The wealth and power of the ruling class remains secure. Religion taught people to accept that their position in society was God's will and that if they behaved properly (i.e. did as the ruling class required, without argument), they would find their reward in the next life (e.g. in heaven).

So, where functionalism sees religion reflecting and promoting collectively agreed norms and values, Marxists see religion promoting the ideology of the dominant ruling class in order to prevent working-class revolution.

Marx was an **atheist**; he believed that God was a product of the human mind. In 1844 he wrote: 'Man makes religion, religion does not make the man' (translated version, Fueur 1984).

Religion, rather than guiding an individual to a higher psychological state, was alienating. In other words it created misery, because it prevented working people from changing their exploited and powerless state of being. Simultaneously, religion acted like a drug, anaesthetising the pain created by this misery.

> Religious distress is at the same time the expression of real distress and the protest against real distress. Religion is the sign of the oppressed creature, the heart of the heartless world, just as it is the spirit of an unspiritual situation. It is the opium of the people.
>
> K. Marx (1844), in L. S. Fruer, *K. Marx and F. Engels: Basic Writings on Politics and Philosophy* (1984)

Religion would disappear, Marx believed, once the social conditions that created the need for it had been overturned. Once the working class became class-conscious (aware of their exploitation and subsequently aware that as a united class they could rise up against the ruling class), they would defeat the ruling class through revolution. Equality (communism) would result. People would no longer feel alienated and, therefore, would have no need for religion.

Neo-Marxists have subsequently tried to clarify how the ruling class use religion to fool the working class. Louis Althusser (1918–1990) followed Marx's assertions relatively closely, but suggested that the various elements of the super-structure, specifically the **ideological state apparatus**, could exist relatively independently of the economic base of inequality, although they were all working towards the same outcome — ruling class control over the working class. He thought that religion was part of the ideological state apparatus because it had direct links with the ruling-class state and its function was the maintenance of ideological control. However, it was not directly influenced by the economy. Jones (2005) notes how the church in feudal times dominated ideological socialisation (rather than the education system, which is the key agent of ideological socialisation in modern capitalism).

Task 2.5

Why might education have taken over from religion as a means of **ideological control** in modern society?

Guidance

Your answer might consider the effect of the declining influence of religion in modern society (**secularisation**).

Marxists argue that the hidden curriculum of schools has replaced the role of religion in teaching respect for authority and appropriate codes of behaviour. In May 2006, Bill Rammell, Minister for Higher Education, announced that children should be taught 'traditional (or core) British values'. The justification for this was that 'the UK is a strong multi-faith society, but to prosper, it must focus on shared core values' (Taylor 2006). This shows the link between education and religion. Marxists would argue that it is not society that would prosper from this, but the ruling class.

Antonio Gramsci (1891–1937), a neo-Marxist who was jailed by the pre-Second World War Italian fascist government for his communist beliefs, argued that religion contributed to the maintenance of hegemony — ideological domination. He was concerned particularly with the role of the Roman Catholic Church in giving ideological support to the fascist state and helping to keep the working class in their exploited position. Gramsci offered a possibility of the working class gaining domination of the ruling ideas in society and using this to reconstruct moral and intellectual leadership to support a revolutionary movement; this could be with the support of religion, but most likely would be without it.

Evaluation of Marxist interpretations

Strengths

Giddens (1993) says: 'Marx is right to claim that religion often has ideological implications serving to justify the interests of ruling groups at the expense of others; there are innumerable instances of this in history.' Giddens offers the examples of Christian imperialism (e.g. the crusades of the Middle Ages and,

Task 2.6

Using history books designed for Key Stage 3 or 4, research some of the examples presented by Giddens (above) to find out exactly how they might justify Marx's claim for the function of religion.

some would argue, the Gulf wars), Christian missionaries and the justification of slavery in the USA during the eighteenth and nineteenth centuries.

We could add to Giddens's list the claim of medieval monarchs (e.g. James I and Charles I) to the divine right of kings, which argued that they were God's representatives on Earth and, therefore, had to be obeyed by all, without question.

Box 2.1

Religious elite

Fenn (2000) claims that the religious 'elite' (leaders), often:

> …seek to own and control access to the sacred. The usual justification for such a monopoly is that such knowledge is too dangerous for the uninitiated and requires someone with the advantages of special training and personal capacity in order to protect the larger society from unpleasant surprises.

This would protect the favoured status of religion as part of the ideological state apparatus.

Religious leaders are closely linked with the state. Note how world political leaders often seek an audience with the Pope; it could be argued that this reciprocally legitimates their elite positions. The British prime minister often meets the Archbishop of Canterbury. There is a close relationship between the Church of England and the House of Lords, which gives it the ability to contribute to the law-making process.

TopFoto

Box 2.2

The Church of England and the House of Lords

The **Anglican** Archbishops of Canterbury and York, the Bishops of Durham, London and Winchester and the 21 senior diocesan bishops of the Church of England have seats in the House. This is because the Church of England is the 'established' **Church** of the State.

House of Lords Briefing Paper, November 2005 (www.parliament.uk)

The Archbishop of Canterbury, Rowan Williams, leaving number 10 Downing Street after a meeting with the Prime Minister, Tony Blair

Limitations

- Some neo-Marxist critics argue that Marxist theories of religion are too economically deterministic. In other words, it is felt that the theory gives too much power to the role of the economy in determining the lives of ordinary people and not enough to other institutions.

- Phenomenologists and postmodernists have criticised the general structural determinism of Marxist interpretations of the functions of religion. Their theories suggest that individuals have a conscious awareness that Marxists seem to deny. People are not passive and do have the capacity to change their world if they want to.
- Some theologians (e.g. Gollwitzer 1970) have claimed that the continuation of religion in societies claiming to be communist — for example Cuba and China, where religion is officially banned yet continues unofficially — suggests that Marx was wrong in his claim that communist revolution did away with the need for religion. They also use this 'fact' to justify the truth of God; the argument suggests that people worship in all societies because there is a fundamental truth in the existence and greatness of God.

Feminists on the functions of religion

As a broad generalisation, feminists see society dominated by men. The essence of this is called patriarchy. Radical feminists take the view that men use physical strength to maintain control over women; Marxist feminists emphasise the role of men using economic power to keep control. Both perspectives take the view that religion is used by men as a tool to maintain control over women; the specific explanations draw on their initial assumptions about the maintenance of patriarchy.

Mary Daly is an important radical feminist writer on the function of religion. Her work *The Church and the Second Sex* (1968) concentrated on misogyny in the Roman Catholic Church. She considers how the book of Genesis in the Old Testament talks of God creating Adam in his own likeness (so men are like God) and then creating Eve (so women are the second sex).

She also argues that the New Testament reinforces the social inferiority of women, particularly in texts emphasised by the Roman Catholic Church. This point has been traced back to Elizabeth Cady Stanton (1895) who, in her *Women's Bible*, argued that God had created men and women equally. The current Bible did not reflect this because it had been written and edited by men to suit their own interpretation. This is a theme taken up more recently in Dan Brown's novel *The Da Vinci Code* (2004), in which it is claimed that the senior figures of the Roman Catholic Church allowed only their own interpretations of the life of Christ to be included in the Bible, a notion that has upset many Christians. However, some commentators outside the Church feel that this fictional claim has a good deal of fact behind it.

> Box 2.3
> **The Da Vinci Code**
>
> Sophie read the passage:
>
> > And the companion of the saviour is Mary Magdelene. Christ loved her more than all the disciples and used to kiss her often on the mouth. The rest of the disciples were offended by it and expressed disapproval. They said to him, 'Why do you love her more than us?'
>
> The woman they are speaking of,' Teabing explained, 'is Mary Magdelene. Peter is jealous of her.'
>
> 'Because Jesus preferred Mary?'
>
> 'Not only that. The stakes were far greater than mere affection. At this point in the gospels, Jesus suspects He will soon be captured and crucified. So He gives Mary Magdelene instructions on how to carry out His Church after He is gone. As a result, Peter expresses his discontent over playing second fiddle to a woman. I daresay Peter was something of a sexist.'
>
> Sophie was trying to keep up. 'This is Saint Peter. The rock on which Jesus built His Church.'
>
> 'The same, except for one catch. According to these unaltered gospels, it was not *Peter* to whom Christ gave directions with which to establish the Christian Church. It was *Mary Magdelene*.'
>
> Sophie looked at him. 'You're saying the Christian Church was to be carried on by a woman?'
>
> 'That was the plan. Jesus was the original feminist. He intended for the future of His Church to be in the hands of Mary Magdelene.'
>
> Source: D. Brown, *The Da Vinci Code* (2004)

Daly presents the argument that the Roman Catholic Church provides the view that men have been given the mission of preaching about God, and that women have the 'mission to listen'. This message is then applied to everyday life, where women are made to do men's bidding. This might be thought of as 'symbolic violence', because it precludes women from exerting their own opinions and personality.

Daly's book *Beyond God the Father* (1978) took a wider look at the use of religion by men to maintain patriarchal control. She argued that patriarchal beliefs and practices are at the core of all the world's religions.

This takes many forms, but the outcome is always the same — male control. Humiliating and physically dangerous (even murderous) practices are used. One

Task 2.7

Read the following extracts from the New Testament. How might Daly use them to reinforce her argument?

Extract 1

...women should keep silence in churches. For they are not permitted to speak, but should be subordinate as even the law says. If there is anything they desire to know, let them ask their husbands at home. For it is shameful for a woman to speak in church. (Corinthians 14:34–35)

Extract 2

Wives, be subject to your husbands as to the Lord. For the husband is the head of the wife as Christ is the head of the church. As the church is subject to Christ, so let wives be the subject in everything to their husbands. (Ephesians 5:22–24)

example of this is the burning of witches or 'hags' by the Christian Church in medieval Europe. Daly refers to a hag as a woman who refused to be passive. Witch hunts were used to persecute women who did not live up to the expectations of men. Some radical feminists have referred to this period as 'the women's Holocaust' because, they assert, so many women were killed. In the Salem witch trials, made famous in Arthur Miller's play *The Crucible* (1952), women avoided being hanged for witchcraft (a crime in the eyes of the church) by accusing others. This allowed men to rule by fear. Daly suggests that 'women are [also] used as token torturers to carry out mutilations. These practices include: foot-binding in ancient China, suttee or widow burning in India, clitoridectomy, or removal of the clitoris, in Africa'.

Task 2.8

Use the internet to investigate one of the above examples of torture in more detail. Can it be justified as male violence (particularly when it is perpetrated by women)?

The Marxist feminist view of the function of religion closely relates to the Marxist view that the state uses religion to oppress people, by legitimating their lack of economic power. Gilbert Achcar, in consideration of Islamic state run societies, argues that:

Women undergo a secular oppression, draped in religious legitimation...One of the most elementary aspects of women's freedom is their individual freedom to dress as they like. When the Islamic scarf and...more enveloping versions of this type of garment, are imposed on women, they are one of the numerous forms of everyday sexual oppression — a form all the more visible as it serves to make women invisible. The struggle against the requirement to wear the scarf or other veils is inseparable from the struggle against other elements of female servitude.

Achcar, www.internationalviewpoint.org/article.php3?id_article=622

Female servitude, through domestic labour, shows the Marxist feminist nature of Achcar's position.

Task 2.9

Read the following extracts taken from an autobiography about life under the Islamist Taliban state (1996–2000) in Afghanistan. Select appropriate evidence to support either the radical or Marxist feminist arguments about the functions of religion.

Extract 1

The new decrees according to **Sharia law** are:

- Girls and women are not allowed to work outside the home.
- All women who have to leave their houses must be accompanied by a **mahram**.
- Women and girls must wear the **burqa**.
- Women and girls are forbidden to wear brightly coloured clothes beneath their burqas.
- Nail polish, lipstick and make-up are forbidden.

Extract 2

But fear among women is now so prevalent that it's becoming second nature. Fear of meeting a neighbour, of answering a question. We're suspicious of everything. I open the door to a brown burqa. The woman pulls it off as soon as the door is shut. Her face is swollen, her lips puffed and bleeding. She doesn't need to speak. I lead her to the living room where my mother examines her. Out of respect, I leave them alone together. But I hear the woman crying through the shut door and a few moments later my mother calls me. 'Bring some boiling water and bandages. Quick'.

I fill a pot, prepare bandages and wait for the trembling of the water impatiently. Yet another woman humiliated and beaten. God only knows why.

I watch mother clean and with a surgical needle sew up the wounds that cover the chest and torso of this woman. A clandestine doctor has to know how to do more or less everything in this mad world of ours. This woman tells us of the latest injustice. She's been whipped by the Taliban's cable — lashes because she dared to go out on her own.

Mother asks her, 'Why did you go out alone?'

Task 2.9 continued

'My father was killed in battle during the winter of 1994. I have no husband, no brother, no son. How am I to live if I can't go out alone?'

Extract 3

During this time, two Afghan women declared guilty of adultery are executed in the Kabul Stadium. Ten unfaithful husbands are whipped.

Extract 4

While the men talked politics, mother, Diba and I could only speak of women, the oppressed who lived without voice or rights, designated victims of a systematic purification. Never again to work, to learn, to be seen.

Source: Latifa (2005) *My Forbidden Face: Growing Up Under the Taliban: a Young Woman's Story*

Evaluation of feminist interpretations

Strengths

Feminist accounts offer logical explanations for the male control of religious hierarchies. The leaders of all the major world religions have been, and continue to be, men. Although women have entered into higher positions in some American Christian churches, they are rare instances. The inclusion of women in religious hierarchies causes controversy. For example:

The General Synod of the Church of England voted in favour of the ordination of women priests in 1992. The first group of 1000 women were ordained in 1994. About 470 male clergy left the church in protest soon after...By 2005, some sources estimated that a total of 720 priests had left.

www.religioustolerance.org/femclrg15

Women are now campaigning for their inclusion as bishops in the Anglican Church.

Limitations

- Theologians and 'ordinary' followers of religions claim that feminists are too generalising and subjective in their claims about patriarchal control — that not all religions are like this. They argue that feminists are selective in their use of examples to support their case, while ignoring examples that could disprove their argument.

- Many Muslims claim that examples like the Taliban are extremely rare and represent a deliberate male misinterpretation of Islam. Men and women are different in the eyes of the religion and both sexes are happy with their assigned roles. This difference should not lead to abuse; this would be morally wrong. Therefore, claims of patriarchy either represent an inadequate knowledge of Islam (or other religions) by white middle-class feminists or a misinterpretation of Islam by groups such as the Taliban.
- Religion may have been patriarchal in the past, but so was society. Both religion and society are now more inclusive of women and the movement to full equality continues. Feminists should therefore update their theories.

Phenomenologists on the functions of religion

Phenomenologists oppose structural theories such as functionalism, Marxism and feminism in their emphasis on the role of institutions like religion in shaping the behaviour of individuals. Rather, they draw upon social action theory in focusing on the religious experience of individuals. Where structural theory tends to see individual adherents as passive and acted upon, phenomenology sees them as actively making decisions about what to believe and how to worship.

Peter Berger is the major phenomenologist contributing to the sociology of religion, although much of his early work is similar to that of Durkheim. Berger believes in God and argues that God is a fundamental truth. However, he believes that the way God is interpreted, and the way religion becomes institutionalised, is down to individuals. Society arises out of the combined choices that individuals make.

Socialisation contributes to this by producing 'taken-for-granted' or 'second nature' ways of acting. Religion is an element of this socialisation. Religions, via human interpretation, create definitions of sacredness. These definitions help to explain the potential chaos beyond human experience and lead to a 'meaningful order'. Ritual helps to reaffirm notions of the sacred.

The difference between these ideas and those of Durkheim is that, whereas Durkheim sees these notions imposed on individuals by the whole group, Berger sees them as individually developed and then shared.

Berger's friend and colleague, Thomas Luckmann, added that even when individuals are socialised into a traditional religious model, they interpret this in their own ways; some will be more religious than others. Individuals accept the 'truth' of the traditional model when public circumstances require it — for example, having a church wedding or gaining access to a church school by convincing the authorities of their commitment. However, their reading of the 'truth' is highly subjective.

Box 2.4

Angel

This theory (subjective interpretation of the 'truth') is illustrated in the following extract, set in the Caribbean island of Grenada where a mother, Doodsie, explains her personal understanding of God to her daughter, Angel. Note how it differs from the view presented by institutionalised religion.

> And then one day, during religious knowledge class in second form, Angel had a rude shock. Mother Superior said that not only was living together without being married a mortal sin, but if a Catholic got married in a non-Catholic church, then that was no marriage and the person and the whole family was living in sin until there was a confession and a repentance and a real marriage in a Catholic church. When Angel got home that day, Doodsie confirmed her fears. Angel went quietly to her room and wept her disappointment.
>
> Later she pleaded with Doodsie to get married to her father again, in the Roman Catholic church. Doodsie laughed.
>
> 'You an you nuns damn awright, you here. Me an God going to sort it out when ah reach up there.'
>
> Angel told Doodsie about mortal sin and hell. Doodsie told her to discuss it with her father. For weeks, Angel tried miserably to persuade her.
>
> 'Look, chile, you doin you bes. God caan vex wid you once you try, so you won't burn for dat. God goin to be really unreasonable if he let you burn too even after you try so hard.'
>
> Angel still looked worried. Doodsie tried to settle it.
>
> 'As for me is awright. I always talkin to God. We have an understanding.'
>
> …'If he dat drastic, I not sure I want to know that type of God.'
>
> Source: M. Collins, *Angel* (1987)

Evaluation of the phenomenological interpretation

Strengths

- Heelas and Woodhead (2001) argue that Berger's theories '...still retain enormous explanatory value. Far more modern men and women now accept the designation "spiritual", rather than "religious". In doing so, they distance themselves from what they perceive to be external, oppressive, inflexible, ritualised, dead and second-hand (i.e. institutionalised) religion'. It may well be that churches have also acknowledged this; some are trying to renew themselves and make themselves more user friendly. The Alpha Course (www.alphacourse.org) and the Emerging Church (www.emergingchurch.info) movement support this argument. These are covered in Chapter 5.

- Postmodernists would also support the notion that individuals interpret their social world in a personal way and, therefore, there are no fixed truths. In the postmodern argument, subjective choice is emphasised when the (potential) adherent acts like a consumer. Hunt (2003) said that: 'Consumerism, with its concern with *taste* and *choice*, means that religion is a matter of personal preference and a product to be packaged for the "spiritual marketplace" of competing religions'.

Limitations

- Modern structural theorists argue that people may decide on their form of religiosity, but can only do so from a limited number of options. Their views are not individually arrived at but determined by structured influences (primarily from religious institutions but also from other structures, such as the family, education and the media).
- Berger has argued that individual religious notions are based on personal understandings of the 'sacred', which subsequently bring order to the lives of people. However, science is also used to bring meaningful order to lives. What makes this different from religion? Where does the sacred end? The criticism here is that Berger and his phenomenological colleagues need to tighten up their definitions and concepts — they need to operationalise their concepts more rigorously. Their argument would be that this is not possible if we want to take individual conceptions into account.

Summary

- Structural theories such as functionalism, Marxism and feminism emphasise the functions religion serves on a societal level.
- Functionalists argue that religion provides society with consensus by acting as:
  - a means of uniting people by bringing them together in ritual and celebration
  - a moral system; norms and values that guide the behaviour patterns of individual members
  - a means of explaining the inexplicable and, therefore, avoiding stress that could disrupt individual lives and the smooth running of society

Task 2.10

Assess the view that, in most societies, religion functions more to cause consensus than to cause conflict.

Guidance

This is structured like a typical AQA question and, therefore, requires a range of skills. You need to:

- show breadth of knowledge and understanding by referring to the main perspectives on the functions of religion
- build in assessment by looking at the strengths and weaknesses of each of the perspectives and by using examples from the religions that you have researched. You could use the quotations from the Bible given in this chapter to support your analysis
- plan the whole essay before you begin writing so that you can interweave knowledge and evaluation points throughout

Explain the approaches of each of the main sociological perspectives — functionalists emphasise consensus, whereas Marxists and feminists stress conflict. Explain the types of research evidence chosen to support their arguments. For example, a functionalist might examine the use of songs and chants in a church or temple to create a shared experience that brings adherents closer together.

The evaluative element of the essay should consider the strengths and weaknesses of each perspective. For example, the functional perspective might fail to explain adequately the conflict that has been prevalent in Northern Ireland between Protestants and Catholics. (Before embarking on this essay, it would be a good idea to read some of the case studies in the next chapter as part of your research.)

The essay should finish with a substantial conclusion that sums up your assessment of the strengths and weaknesses of each perspective. Is a consensus or conflict approach more accurate in the assessment of the role of religion? Which do you think offers the way forward? Ideally, do not sit on the fence and say that you can see the merits of all; opt for one if you can. This, if properly justified with good reasons, would earn more marks for evaluation. However, if you feel particularly strongly one way or the other it is easy to be too dogmatic and, consequently, fail to give adequate academic justifications — so be careful.

- The key function of religion for Marx was the creation of false class-consciousness. This is a condition in the minds of working-class people that their position at the bottom of society is fair and appropriate. As a result, they do not feel exploited and, therefore, do not rise up against the ruling class.

- Feminists take the view that religion is used by men as a tool to maintain control over women. Specific explanations draw on the initial assumptions that have been made about the maintenance of patriarchy.
- Where structural theories tend to see individual adherents as passive and acted upon by religious institutions, phenomenologists see people as actively making decisions, or subjective interpretations, about what to believe and how to worship.

Research suggestions

- You might approach a local church, mosque, synagogue or temple to ask if you could research, via questionnaire or interview, why its members attend and what they feel their religion gives them. Which sociological perspective is supported by the answers you gain? You will need to have researched a good deal about the religion beforehand so that your questions are deemed by the respondents to be worthwhile. You will also need to be ethically aware: seek the support of your teacher/lecturer in checking over your question-naire/interview plan — before you even pilot it — to ensure that no-one will be offended by it.
- You could test Bellah's concept of civil religion by asking people, through a questionnaire or interview, what they can remember about Millennium or World Cup 'celebrations'. What did it do for them as individuals? What do they think it did for society?
- You could interview a number of teachers and ask them whether they think it is possible consciously to teach a core of shared values in modern society and in what ways they think it could be, or is, done? Do their answers reflect points from a particular perspective?

Useful websites

- www.bytrent.demon.co.uk/durkheim1.html
  This site carries a relatively detailed examination of Durkheim's theory of the sacred and of the functions of religion.
- http://en.wikipedia.org/wiki/sociology_of_religion
  This site has a section on the key classical theories of the sociology of religion and a useful glossary.
- http://womenshistory.about.com/od/quotes/a/mary_daly.htm
  This site has a collection of interesting quotes from the radical feminist Mary Daly; first-hand extracts, but quite short and accessible.

Further reading

- Haralambos, M. et al. (1987) *Sociology: A New Approach*, Causeway Press.
  This book was written for GCSE students. It contains two excellent articles on

the functions of religion — first, from a functionalist perspective, looking at the work of Malinowski and second, from a Marxist perspective, using the example of gospel singers. Each article finishes with some useful exercises.

- Kidd, W. et al. (1998) *Readings in Sociology*, Heinemann.

This book of selected first-hand extracts includes readings from Durkheim, Marx and Berger. The section on religion, and each reading, has a brief introduction to help you, plus glossaries and questions.

Religion and social change

Does religion prevent or cause social change?

Functionalists, Marxists and feminists argue that religion functions to keep society stable; in other words, it prevents change. However, the German Max Weber (1864–1920) saw religion as contributing to social change. He identified a link between the branch of Christian Protestantism called Calvinism and the development of capitalism in western Europe. In recent times, there have been arguments about whether Islamic fundamentalism is trying to take the world back to a non-industrial past or trying to give the world a totally Islamic future. Others have accused the Roman Catholic Church of trying to prevent social and medical progress. This chapter aims to lead you through these arguments.

A brief guide to Christianity

In order to understand much of the work on the sociology of religion, in particular the work of Weber, it is important to understand how Christianity has developed. Most of the sociology you need to know has a British (and, some would say, ethnocentric) bias. Therefore, if you are unclear about this religious history, much of the sociology will make little sense.

It may be that you have been brought up in a Christian family or community and have a good grasp of Christian beliefs. If so, you can afford to skim-read this section. However, you should make sure that you understand what the different branches of Christianity stand for. If you have not been brought up in the Christian tradition and, particularly, if you were a student who complained about having to study religious education and history at Key Stage 3 (and therefore didn't listen), you need to read this carefully.

Christians believe that Jesus Christ was the Son of God. They believe that God sent him to save them from the evil caused by the sins of Adam and Eve and all human beings since. Jesus was born to Mary and Joseph (remember the nativity plays from primary school?). Mary had conceived by Immaculate Conception; God had made her pregnant by his super-empirical powers rather than by the usual method. This was one way of showing that, although Jesus had a human form, he was not a human being.

As an adult, Jesus set out to spread the word of God. He travelled through Palestine/Israel preaching and performing miracles to 'prove' his claim to be the Son of God. As he travelled he gathered a number of (male) followers who are known as the disciples.

At his last supper (John 13–16), which is remembered on Maundy Thursday, the Bible tells us that Jesus gave his disciples the mission of continuing his task of spreading the word of God. Jesus told them that they would be guided by the Holy Spirit, which would help them speak to people of other languages. He also told them that he needed to die in order to come back later to save the world (John 16). These are central themes for Pentecostalists, who believe that good Christians are able to speak 'in tongues'. Some Christians believe in following the disciples and taking the message of Jesus directly to the non-Christian world, so that it can join in the benefits of believing in Christ. Such Christians are of many different branches of the faith, but are generally known as evangelicals. Some of these (such as Jehovah's Witnesses) focus their beliefs and activities on the second coming of Christ (predicted by Jesus in John 16); this approach is known as millenarian. One disciple, Peter, was chosen to be the lead disciple whose specific mission was to set up a formal church.

Jesus was arrested for treason by the Romans who ruled Israel at this time and, on Good Friday, he was crucified (John 19). This is why the cross has become a sacred symbol for Christians. As the Son of God, he could, of course, have used his powers to avoid this painful end. However, he chose not to in order to show his commitment to human kind. The 'dead' body of Christ was laid in a tomb and closed by a large rock that took many men to move. On Easter Sunday, Jesus rose from the dead and was later to take his place next to God in heaven (on Ascension Day). There were other examples of his transcendent powers.

The disciples were able to use the communications networks created by the Roman Empire to spread the word of Christ. Initially, life was not easy for them or their converts. The Romans saw them as dangerous to their rule and persecuted them. You may have heard the stories of Christians being fed to the lions by Romans for entertainment. The first recorded English martyr was St Alban, a Roman soldier who had converted to Christianity. The town and abbey that bear his name record the site of this event. Christians at this time used the Greek word 'ichthys' as an acronym for the Greek words representing 'Jesus Christ, Son of God, Saviour'. They used the symbol of a

The ichthys symbol on a car reveals the owner's Christian beliefs

fish, rather than a cross, to let other like-minded people know of their sacred beliefs, because this avoided detection by the Romans. Today, you may see this symbol used on cars, where Christians exhibit their belief to others.

The official persecution of Christians by the Romans came to an end in the fourth century AD. The religion became acceptable and over a period of years the formal church became based in Rome. This church became known as the Church of Rome and later the Roman Catholic Church. The site of this is the Vatican City, which is the home of the leader of the Roman Catholic Church, the Pope. It has been argued that the first Christian church was built in Glastonbury (where the music festival now takes place) between AD 37 and 63 (www.isleofavalon.co.uk/history/antiquity.html) because, at that time, England was a safe place for Christians to worship.

The subsequent progress of Christianity is characterised by periodic conflicts about the exact message of Jesus Christ and God, how God should be worshipped and where the home of the church should be.

In the eleventh century there was a schism (break) between those who believed that the home of the church should be in Rome and those who thought it should be in Constantinople. (The reasons for this are beyond the scope of this book.) It led to the setting up of the Orthodox (Coptic) Church, which is most firmly established in Greece, Cyprus and eastern European countries, such as Russia. As an 'orthodox' church, it claims to be closer to the original version of Christianity.

In the sixteenth century, a number of Christians, including John Calvin (a Frenchman domiciled in Geneva) and Martin Luther (a German), criticised the Roman Church for being hypocritical and decadent. While the Church told its adherents to help the poor and live a simple life as Jesus had done (and argued that others should do), these critics argued that church leaders lived in the finest houses, wore the finest clothes and ate the finest foods. The *protests* led by these critics resulted in the formation of a new interpretation of Christianity, known as Protestantism. However, there were various local interpretations of exactly what a Protestant Church should stand for. In England, the Protestant movement was hijacked by Henry VIII. He used it to set up the Church of England, which he then headed. This meant that he did not have to take account of the authority of the Pope, therefore making himself more powerful. He could also divorce his first wife.

One of the Protestant arguments was that the word of God should be brought closer to ordinary people. James I did this, as head of the Church of England, by having the Latin Bible of the Catholic Church translated into English.

However, some Protestants were not happy about the monarch heading the new Protestant Church. Their argument was that the nature of the religion had not changed by substituting the king for the Pope. They believed the argument for the divine right of kings to be an outrage. Only God could be head of the Church. As a result, they sought a much flatter hierarchical structure. The fundamental beliefs and practices needed to come closer to the 'pure' form of Christianity; such Protestants were therefore called Puritans. They demanded that adherents should eat simple food, and not drink alcohol, gamble, dance or go to the theatre. Sex should be kept within marriage. They should not work on Sundays, which should be devoted to God, as he demanded in the Ten Commandments (Exodus 20). Under pressure from prosecution and persecution for failing to accept the commands of the king, many Puritans emigrated to North America. These Puritans are the ancestors of the New (Christian fundamentalist) Right in the USA.

In the UK, the descendants of the Puritans formed protestant denominations, for example the Baptist Church, Methodism, the United Reformed Church, the Congregational Church and the Presbyterian Church. These branches of Protestantism became known as nonconformist churches, because they refused to conform to the will of the monarch (and the state to which the monarch was closely linked); they also became associated with the poorer people.

Task 3.1

Look for evidence of Protestant nonconformist churches in your local town. You will find that, in general, compared with the Anglican churches they are much smaller and less ornate. If you take a walk inside nonconformist churches you would find no statues; the view is that there should be nothing to distract the believer from concentrating on the word of God.

Box 3.1

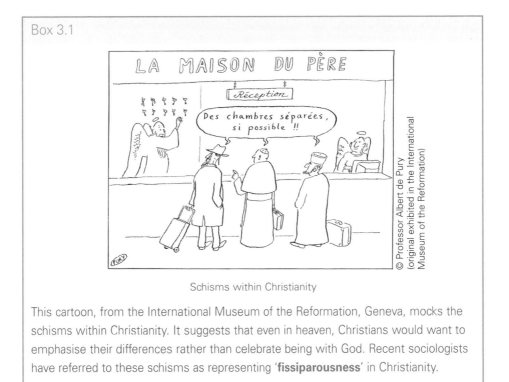

© Professor Albert de Pury
(original exhibited in the International
Museum of the Reformation)

Schisms within Christianity

This cartoon, from the International Museum of the Reformation, Geneva, mocks the schisms within Christianity. It suggests that even in heaven, Christians would want to emphasise their differences rather than celebrate being with God. Recent sociologists have referred to these schisms as representing '**fissiparousness**' in Christianity.

In the present day, there are probably as many differences within Catholicism and Protestantism as there are between them, as both branches of Christianity struggle to find new ways to enthuse members. The key differences are summed up as follows:

- Roman Catholicism predominates in southern European countries such as Italy, Spain and Portugal; also in southern Ireland.
- Catholics give a fairly central role to the Virgin Mary, who was the mother of God. She offers particular guidance to women.
- Catholics also give more emphasis on saints, i.e. people who have led particularly good lives and have been formally recognised (canonised) as having done so; they are role models for Catholics.
- Catholic churches are usually ornate. They make use of pictures and statues (or icons) to deliver specific messages.
- Catholics take their guidance from the Pope. Church of England members take their lead from the Archbishop of Canterbury; the monarch is now a figurehead only. The nonconformist churches are much less strict than they used to be and more democratic than the other churches. They often rely on guidance from local leaders.

Task 3.2

Summarise this account of the historical development of Christianity in the form of a time-line. Representing the key events in both pictures and words may help you to remember it.

How functionalists explain the link

The functionalist argument is that religion supports evolutionary change and prevents rapid or revolutionary change. Functionalists take the view that society evolves in much the same way that Darwinians say that species have evolved. They think that this imperceptible change ensures the maintenance of social stability. Religion is just one of many institutions that ensure such evolutionary change.

Continued stability and evolutionary change are illustrated with reference to the organic analogy. The argument is that the institutions of society — for example religion — function in a similar way to the organs of the human body (e.g. heart, lungs), in that the organs are interdependent but each has a specific function. According to functionalists such as Durkheim, religion acts in much the same way. Functionalists see religion as equivalent to the healthy heart, providing society with the strength to continue by providing norms, values and an explanation for the normally inexplicable. Religion could evolve to suit new situations. For example, some societies are predominantly Christian; others are Islamic or Hindu. Religion could, theoretically, fail in its present form, but be 'transplanted' (or supported) through the use of functional equivalents such as civil religion or football. As long as people in society were provided with 'spiritual guidance', the source would not really matter, provided that change was gradual.

Evaluation

- You could use Alpha Courses and the Emerging Church movement (see Chapter 5) as examples of the evolution of institutionalised Christianity to meet the needs of a postmodern or postindustrial society.
- A specific criticism of the functionalist view is that it fails to note examples of societies undergoing radical social change supported by religion (e.g. Iran).
- There are several general criticisms of functionalist theories of religion in Chapter 2 (p. 21).

In Task 3.3 (below), following the section on Marxists, some examples that could be used to evaluate both perspectives are considered.

How Marxists explain the link

Marxists argue that the main function of religion is to inhibit (or hinder) social change. The ruling classes use religion to help them make the working class falsely class conscious. Religion encourages good behaviour; a level of satisfaction with what they have now and a belief that their good behaviour will be rewarded in the 'next life' by their God(s). As a result, working-class people do not realise that they are being exploited by the ruling class, or that by joining together, they could rise up and defeat the ruling class. Consequently, the powerful and privileged position of the ruling class remains safe. Reference to Marxists in an answer on religion and social change should develop these ideas and include the ideas of Marx, Althusser and Gramsci (see Chapter 2).

Evaluation

General criticisms of Marxist theories of religion are covered in Chapter 2 (pp. 24–26). A specific criticism of the traditional Marxist view that religion inhibits social change comes from the neo-Marxist, Otto Maduro (1982). He argues that religion in some societies has been used to lead social change by taking the side of the oppressed working class. Clearly, if a Christian Church responded to Jesus's quote about the camel and the eye of a needle — 'it is easier for a camel to go through the eye of a needle than for a rich man to enter the kingdom of God' — then there is an argument for supporting any change that helps to make the distribution of wealth more equal.

Task 3.3

Consider the following observations on the Roman Catholic Church. How far could they be used to support or refute functionalist and Marxist arguments about religion as an inhibitor of social change?

Roman Catholicism: a creator or inhibitor of social change?

Roman Catholicism is one of the world's major religions. It has 1.1 billion adherents. How far has its theology impacted on the people who follow it and on the places where they live? Does it encourage or hinder change?

Task 3.3 continued

Between the 1950s and the 1970s, Latin American Roman Catholic leaders and priests developed and promoted what they called liberation theology, which combined Christian ethics with Marxist political theory. The fundamental argument was that Jesus was a revolutionary who was aiming to free the poor from oppression. Therefore, present-day Catholics should do the same by helping to free workers from the exploitation of capitalism. An example of liberation theology in action was the Sandinista revolution in Nicaragua, Central America (1979). The Sandinistas, with the support of the people and Catholic Church in Nicaragua, defeated the state dictatorship.

A similar situation occurred in the early 1980s in the Philippines, where a corrupt government led by Ferdinand Marcos and supported by the USA had quashed the opposition. When a popular opposition leader was assassinated, the national Catholic leader, Cardinal Sin, openly criticised Marcos and supported the opposition movement. After another corrupt election, Sin called for widespread opposition. The people responded with several days of street-based demonstrations. This ended when Marcos fled the country.

Polish-born Pope John Paul II is seen to have played a significant part in the uprising, in 1989, by the people of Poland against the communist government imposed on them following the Second World War. Hooper (2005) and Langley (2005), among others, note how he gave moral (and possibly financial) support to the trade union movement 'Solidarity', which led the protests. Langley goes as far as arguing that Solidarity was Pope Jean Paul's 'special inspiration'.

Despite the Pope's contribution to changing regimes in Haiti and Poland, Khan (2005) notes how John Paul II was a strongly conservative leader, who encouraged Catholics to reject social and technological developments. He led arguments against abortion, stem-cell research and euthanasia (even in extreme circumstances, as in the case of the removal of a feeding tube from an American woman who had been in a coma for 15 years). He was strongly opposed to the ordination of women despite 'the potentially crippling shortage of priests' (Khan 2005). This led to a rift with the Church of England, which was ordaining women. John Paul's opposition to the use of condoms led to much criticism, particularly from AIDS charities concerned about the spread of HIV and AIDS in developing Catholic countries.

Other commentaries have noted how the present Pope, Benedict XVI (previously Cardinal Ratzinger) led a campaign to silence or sideline senior liberation theologians 'forbidding them to teach or preach' (Stanford 2006). Some were allowed to continue as long as they taught the truth about Christ 'without Marxist interpretations' (*New Internationalist* 2000). Some people are hopeful that Benedict will allow some

Task 3.3 continued

change, but Stanford argues that his election is 'a fatal blow to the hopes of all those who argued that the church needed to update its view…'. His past record and age suggest that change is unlikely.

Guidance
Your answer should indicate that Catholicism has a mixed record. There are examples of it encouraging people to change their circumstances and examples of it hindering social and medical advances. There is evidence to support and to refute both functionalist and Marxist theories.

How Weber explained the link

Max Weber (1864–1920) was one of the originators of sociology (along with Durkheim and Marx). The key emphasis of Weber's theory has been long debated. One interpretation is that religion (in the form of Protestantism) led to the individual beliefs and actions (the Protestant ethic) that gave rise to the development of a new form of society (capitalism). Another, stronger, interpretation argues that Protestantism was the 'inspirational drive' in the creation of capitalism (Parkin 1982), showing that religion can lead to social change.

Weber focused his consideration of Protestantism on Calvinism. It was a strict, nonconformist type of Protestantism, which argued that:

- people should live simply (as Jesus had done), work hard for six days a week and give the seventh day to God (reflecting the advice in the Old Testament book of Genesis). Weber called this the 'Protestant work ethic'. This led Protestants who developed businesses to invest in the enterprise rather than living lavishly off the profits (as 'hypocritical' Catholics were seen to do).
- God helps those who help themselves — reliance on charity or giving to charity was against God's will. Weber argued that this led (via investment of profits in the business) to job creation (rather than giving money to the poor). It allowed the poor to work and to help themselves, while expanding industry.
- God had already chosen the 'elect', i.e. the people he would take into heaven. Catholics believe that living a good life ensures that God will select them to live with him in heaven. This feeling is made more certain by 'confession', in which Catholics admit their sins to God's representative on Earth (the priest) and offer their repentance. This and the 'last rites' (the prayers offered by Catholic priests for the dying) mean that they have made their peace with God, and acceptance into heaven will be guaranteed. Calvanist Protestants had

no confession and no certainty that they would go to heaven. This led to what Weber called salvation anxiety — a state of stress about whether heaven or hell awaited them. Therefore, Calvinists sought signs that God had chosen them. Business success was seen as a major sign of being 'elect' (or chosen). It reinforced the Protestant work ethic and helped to create what Weber called the spirit of capitalism. It was a psychological impetus to ensure that individuals who were motivated by enterprise collectively created industrial capitalism.

Task 3.4

Go to www.newgenevacenter.org/01_Western-Culture-to-1900/11_Religious-Reformation/11_Religious-Reformation.htm for a brief explanation of the growth of Calvinism. What ideas were most important to the countries that adopted Calvinism?

Weber argued that the Protestant ethic was not found elsewhere. So, for example, although China had the right structural conditions (e.g. bureaucratic ways of working) to support the development of capitalism, it lacked the motivational spirit. Its major religion (Confucianism) encouraged adjustment to, rather than mastery or transformation of, the natural world.

Evaluation

Strengths

Jones (1996) argues that Weber's work 'has surprising relevance for contemporary society'. She argues that we can see evidence of the Protestant ethic in the compulsive 'workaholic' nature of present-day society. Many people work more than is wise for their health. This is due partly to their work circumstances, but also to their need for signs of success. It was this latter element that Calvinist Protestants took to be evidence of 'election'. In a secularised world, this is not a likely desire in the minds of the workforce. However, it may well be that the desire to leave their mark on the world is a residue of the Protestant ethic.

Some people feel the need to work too hard, which can lead to poor health

Ultimately, the value of Weber's work is that it shows that actions are determined not only by structural influences, as argued by Durkheim and Marx, but by the goals and motivations of individuals (Swingewood 1999).

Limitations

- Among others, Parkin (1982) argued that the late development of capitalism in Scotland, despite its strong adherence to Calvinism, is evidence that Weber was wrong about the Protestant ethic. Bruce (1996) and Marshall (1980) both argue that despite the existence of the spirit of capitalism through Calvinism, Scotland lacked other conditions necessary for the development of a capitalist economy, such as a developed financial system, good communication and transport and advanced raw material extraction. Critics such as Parkin may not, therefore, have a cast-iron case. However, it is Parkin's assertion that 'it is doubtful whether conditions north of the border were really so different from those in the south'.
- Bruce (1996) and Hamilton (2001) suggest that Weber's theory lacks validity and was based on assumption, rather than evidence. Although there is a case for arguing that Puritan leaders exhibited the 'spirit of capitalism', they believe there is no evidence that their congregations internalised and acted on these messages — 'assuming and knowing are not the same thing' (Bruce 1996). This links with an argument that Weber mistook correlation for causation. In other words, it may be true that Calvinism and capitalism arose at the same time (correlation) but there is little evidence that Calvinism helped to create capitalism.

Are millennial movements forces for social change?

Millennial movements are religious movements that are focused on the creation of a heavenly, perfect place on Earth, one where all people will be equal and have 'peace, justice and plenty' (Hamilton 2001). They have most frequently been found in the developing world. Hamilton notes how Marx and Engels had considered the possibility that they could be vehicles for political protest and, therefore, social change. Engels (1820–95) focused on **millennialism** in Germany during the Middle Ages. He believed that the Protestant Martin Luther had encouraged peasants to campaign to break away from the Catholic Church but that that he had abandoned them when they took their protests for change 'too far'. The interests of the peasants were taken up by Thomas Müntzer and a millennial sect called the Anabaptists. Many (unsuccessful) peasant uprisings, inspired by Müntzer, took place in the search for greater equality and the establishment of the 'kingdom of God'. Hamilton argues that Engels saw Müntzer:

> ...as a hero and a martyr and one of the first revolutionary figures to promote class war... In this way Engels founded the tradition of interpreting millennial movements as...political movements with a class basis and as forerunners of modern class-conscious revolutionary political movements.
>
> Hamilton, *The Sociology of Religion* (2005)

So although millennial movements might push for social change, for Marx and Engels such agendas would fail because they were inspired by religion and, therefore, by false class-consciousness. However, Hamilton takes the view that even consideration of millennial movements by Engels as inspiring protest against the ruling class is contradictory to the underlying premise of religion as an opiate of the masses.

Worsley (1970) shared a similar view to Marx and Engels, seeing millennial movements in the developing world as political reactions to **colonisation**, at least in their early years; they may later run out of revolutionary momentum. However, Cohn (1970) was critical of the view that millennial movements might be seen as political movements for change, regarding them as movements based on fantasy. Cohn did, however, acknowledge that Müntzer's movement was able to achieve limited gains for the peasants.

Hamilton concludes that:

> Millennial movements may be fantastical in their ideas and outlook but they do create the concept of change in cultures that had never before looked at the world as changing and changeable. In time, such a radically new way of thinking can give rise to realistic and rational demands for change based upon an appropriate comprehension of the situation.
>
> Hamilton (2005)

Does Islamic fundamentalism lead to social change?

Fundamentalist groups of any persuasion are of the opinion that their interpretation of the holy text is correct and all others are wrong. They demand strict adherence to what are identified as the key principles or rules. Islamic fundamentalists believe that the Koran is the true word of God and is, therefore, unquestionable. This belief makes them critical of non-fundamentalist Muslims (the vast majority), who do not subscribe to this view and who are seen as too secularist or westernised. Bruce (2000) argues that such interpretations are based on a 'selectively imagined past' in which life was perfect. Sivan (1985) argues that Islamic fundamentalism 'is essentially defensive; a sort of holding operation against modernity'.

The origins of Islamic fundamentalism are a source of academic debate. However, a range of specific events, often in combination, is suggested:

- Islam was the predominant religious and military power in much of southern Europe and north Africa between the eighth and tenth centuries. By the sixteenth century, it had spread as far as Hungary and Austria. Retreat was caused by Christian forces, thus making Christians an old enemy. Any growth of western influence can be labelled as 'Christian aggression' or expansionism.
- Islam (fundamentalist or otherwise) sees itself as the only true religion. It also claims places as sacred in its own terms that are also claimed as sacred by others, such as Jews and Christians. Both these facts are 'a recipe for conflict' (Bruce 2000).
- A major region of conflict is Israel. Islamic fundamentalists argue that it is an artificial nation imposed on indigenous Muslims (the Palestinians) by western nations such as the USA and UK (at best, to appease their consciences for the Holocaust and, at worst, to be aggressive to Islam). Israel is seen by fundamentalists to have seized extra land unlawfully during the Six Day War in 1967 and the Yom Kippur War in 1973. The west failed to prevent this happening and it has remained a source of constant irritation for Muslims who want all 'Islamic land' returned to the Muslims to whom it 'belongs'. However, the Jews see Israel as a land promised by God and argue that much of the land in their possession was sold to them by Arabs. There are two sides to this story.
- The Islamic revolution in Iran (1979) was led by Islamic clerics, in particular Ayatollah Khomeini. The previous regime, under the Shah (monarch) was seen to be backed by western nations — it was viewed as corrupt and exploitative of local Muslims. The revolutionary government imposed Islamic (Shariah) law and its success gave Islamic fundamentalists the confidence and desire to spread the Islamic revolution across the world and to defeat western ideas and influence (hegemony). Subsequently, Afghanistan fell to Islamic fundamentalists, the Taliban (pp. 29–30). The defeat of the Taliban by western forces has reinforced the belief of Islamic fundamentalists that the west wants to quash Islam.

Task 3.5

Given these origins, do you think Islamic fundamentalism is a conservative force or one promoting change? Give reasons for your answer.

The question about whether Islamic fundamentalism is inhibiting or promoting social change is difficult. It appears to be promoting social change, but is also seen to be against modernisation. The events of 9/11 and 7/7 (among others) brought to the attention of the world the beliefs of extreme Islamists, in particular their disgust with western capitalism.

The 9/11 attacks on New York, where two hijacked planes crashed and destroyed the World Trade Center and the remains of the double-decker bus in Tavistock Square after the 7/7 attacks on London

For many, these events represented religion aiming to halt social change (or 'modernisation'). Bruce (2000) argues that fundamentalism of any persuasion is a response to social change — an attempt to reinforce a culture under attack from modernising pressures. However, 'their conservatism is not conservation, but a creative reworking of the past for present purposes'. In other words, they are not aiming to inhibit social change, but to mould it according to their perceived needs.

Tibi (2005) argues that Islamic fundamentalism seeks to employ the benefits of modern science, but to destroy the western cultural values that go with it. It aims to spread the impact of Islam while seeking to return Islam to its perceived roots. He argues that there can be no simple answers to the social change question because different Islamic societies, Islamic fundamentalists and 'ordinary' adherents all have their own understandings of the aim of fundamentalism. It also depends on the nature and speed of future (external) globalising influences and how they are received.

Looking forward, Bruce (2000) argues that western influence will prove to be too powerful and attractive. Although Islamic fundamentalism may still be supported to some extent by poor Muslims, he believes that its activists will be unable to sustain their revolutionary zeal. However, he does suggest that all religions will ultimately fall to secularisation; there are many others who disagree.

Task 3.6

Over the next 2 weeks, track the development of news stories from the Middle East and the Far East. How often do references to Islamic fundamentalism appear and in what form? Is there any evidence for the views of Islamic fundamentalists promoting or hindering social change? How would the sociologists referenced in this chapter explain these events?

Summary

- The functionalist argument is that religion supports evolutionary change and prevents rapid or revolutionary change.
- The Marxist argument is that the main function of a religion is to inhibit (or hinder) social change so that the ruling class can maintain its control over the working class.
- Neo-Marxist Otto Maduro (1982) argued that, in some societies, religious movements — for example liberation theology — have been used to lead social change by taking the side of the oppressed working class.
- Pope John Paul II was a conservative leader who encouraged Catholics to reject social and technological developments. This supports traditional functionalist and Marxist theories.
- The 'strongest' interpretation of Weber's theory argues that Protestantism was the 'inspirational drive' in the creation of capitalism, i.e. that religion led to social change.
- Engels, a Marxist, considered the possibility that millenarian movements could be vehicles for political protest and, therefore, social change.
- Islamic fundamentalists can be seen to advocate a return to the past, a halt to any further change or a move forward (if it embraces Islamic law and culture); it depends on the perspective taken.

Does religion inhibit or promote social change?

Students of sociology know that there is rarely a simple 'right' or 'wrong' answer to any question. This is particularly the case in the area of religion and social change. It is possible to argue that religion can both hinder and promote social change, and it is possible to find examples to support both standpoints. Often they can support both — for example, Islamic fundamentalism promoted the revolution in Iran but has since promoted social stability.

The last word should go to Bruce, who sums up effectively when he argues the following:

> Religious revolts and reformations and revivals may be crushed by the establishment, or they may succeed and become the new establishment. Either way, the fire burns out and there follows a period of calm; until the next wave of enthusiasm.
>
> Bruce, *Fundamentalism* (2000)

Task 3.7

Outline and discuss the view that religion is a force for social change.

Guidance

If you have examples to illustrate each scenario and can place them in a theoretical framework, you will be able to write a strong essay.

This is structured like a typical examination question and, therefore, requires a range of skills. You need to:

- show breadth of knowledge and understanding by referring to the arguments that religion hinders or promotes social change
- build in evaluation by looking at the strengths and weaknesses of both sets of arguments. The case studies of Roman Catholicism, the Protestant ethic, millennial movements and Islamic fundamentalism will help you to do this
- plan the whole essay before you begin writing so that you can interweave knowledge and evaluation points throughout

You should explain what is meant by social change and how religion may hinder or promote it, making reference to the arguments of functionalism, Marxism (including neo-Marxism) and Weber (the Protestant ethic).

The evaluative element of this essay should weigh up the strengths and weaknesses of each of these approaches using a few general criticisms, but mostly by questioning what the case studies cited above tell us about change.

The essay should conclude by summing up the strengths and limitations of the different arguments. Having completed this chapter and perhaps some extension reading, you might have a specific argument in mind. However, there is scope for a sit-on-the-fence conclusion: when society is stable, religion appears to inhibit change, but in times of instability it can be used, alongside other factors, as a focus for change. In other words, religion can either inhibit or promote social change, depending upon the particular circumstances.

Research suggestions

- Use a questionnaire to ask people whether they feel that Islamic fundamentalists will change the world in accordance with their views. How far are people aware of events in regions such as the Middle East, the Far East and Afghanistan? What are their views on the events there? Is Islamic terrorism having an effect on their work and leisure time? Does it affect what they do and where they go?

- If there are Muslim students in your school or college, you could conduct some in-depth interviews to focus on their views of Islamic fundamentalism. Do they think fundamentalists are justified in their criticisms of the west and of non-fundamentalist Muslims? How far have their lives been affected by fundamentalism and other people's reactions to it? You will need to be *extremely* sensitive with your questioning and be prepared to hear views with which you disagree, without arguing back.

Useful websites

- www.quia.com/quiz/317523.html
  This site is a quiz on religion and social change. How much have you learnt?
- www.homestead.com/rouncefield/files/a_soc_rel_1.htm
  This site is a wide-ranging outline of the key theories of religion and social change. The rouncefield home page is also worth visiting for other areas of religion.

Further reading

- Bruce, S. (2000) *Fundamentalism*, Polity.
  This book is concise and is a relatively easy guide to Islamic and Christian fundamentalism, offering historical background and analysis. It will enable you to think about whether fundamentalism is conservative or promotes change.
- Hamilton, M. (2001) *The Sociology of Religion*, Routledge.
  This book carries a more developed account of Weber's Protestant ethic theory than can be offered here, and an interesting account of millenarian movements.

Secularisation

Operationalising the concept: why do definitions matter?

Chapter 1 opened with the claim that the way we define concepts (in that case, religion) affects what we find. Wilson (1966) defined secularisation as '…a process whereby religious thinking, practice and institutions lose social significance'. This quotation gives us a general idea about the nature of secularisation. However, what exactly did he mean by religious thinking, religious practice, religious institutions and social significance? More definitions are required. We have already found that classical sociologists, such as Durkheim, Marx and Weber, saw ideas in society changing as it modernised, and that an implicit part of the general process of social evolution was the progressive decline of formal religion. However, were their predictions correct? Did religion decline, and if it did, has the decline continued?

Whether or not we see a decline in the influence and extent of religion may depend on the definition of religion we start with.

Most sociologists studying secularisation use a substantive definition that focuses on institutionalised religions such as Christianity. They probably see a decrease in membership and attendance. Some such as Bruce (2002) conclude a decline of religion — secularisation.

However Bellah (1967) suggests that 'what is generally called secularisation and the decline of religion appears as the decline of the external control system of religion and the decline of traditional religious beliefs'. He believes that we need to modernise the way we view religiosity — religion is no longer necessarily delivered via formal institutions.

There is an argument for religion being adapted in a personal sense and operating at a more individual level. If we want to know if religion is in decline, we need to ask individuals what gives their lives meaning, what guidance they seek and from where. This is a theme taken up by contemporary sociologists such as Grace Davie.

A functional definition of religion could be used to build on Bellah's argument. It would probably result in seeing religion changing, rather than declining. For example, people may not go to church in the numbers they did 100 years ago, but their lives are still guided — albeit by thoughts and actions of a different kind, perhaps by following a music or football culture. Most sociologists believe that such a broad definition is too general to be useful and have concentrated on definitions of a more substantive nature, although there are still disagreements about what is and is not 'religion'.

Fundamentally, there is a level of subjectivity involved in the search for secularisation. Personal bias affects the selection of definitions for secularisation and religion. Of course, most sociologists would claim to be totally objective, but in the end they will have been guided by their specific perspectives and motives. This ensures that you will always have a specific evaluative point to offer in your answers on secularisation.

With no agreement on definitions of religion or secularisation, how can I understand the debate?

The first step in answering this question is to decide how sociologists should measure religiosity, because this will provide evidence as to whether secularisation is taking place.

Task 4.1

If we were to measure the decline of religiosity (i.e. how people behave in a religious manner) what factors could we look at? Brainstorm a list of indicators of religiousness. Once you have done that, aim to identify the strengths and weaknesses of each item.

For example, an indicator of religiosity might be the number of people getting married in a church. This could suggest that people wanted their marriage to be recognised by God. A strength of this as an indicator of religiosity is that the figures can be found easily. A weakness is that many people get married in a church because it looks nice in the photographs and not because they believe in God. People who do not get married in a church may actually believe in God but might have been refused a church wedding because one or both has been divorced.

What might your list tell you about measuring the decline of religion?

You may have considered the numbers of people who:
- are members of a religion
- attend a place of worship
- say prayers at home
- think their lives are guided by holy books
- believe in heaven (or equivalent)

Statistics on some of these are easier to gain than others. Some rely on people providing truthful answers in surveys. However, on a controversial issue like religion, some people may give the answer they think is expected, rather than the truth. Others rely on churches providing accurate statistics, but churches have obvious reasons to overestimate numbers.

Task 4.2

Go to www.christian-research.org.uk. It has a range of up-to-date statistics on religiosity in Christian churches. What does the organisation appear to say about trends in religiosity? *Sign up for its regular e-mail newsletter.* It will keep you thinking about the key ideas raised in this chapter and will serve as useful revision.

Recently, British sociologists seem to have accepted that there has been a decline in the indicators of religiosity associated with formal or institutionalised religion, such as attendance at church services and the number of baptisms and church weddings. Some sociologists argue that statistics on the decline of institutionalised religion are enough to indicate that religion is no longer significant. Others argue that the statistics suggest disillusionment with organised religion, but that people are privately still religious; religiosity has changed rather than disappeared.

It would be impossible for you to know all the work carried out on secularisation, so this chapter concentrates on four key theorists: Wilson and Bruce, who are sure of the occurrence of secularisation (at least in Britain); and Martin and Davie, who have questioned this certainty. For each set of arguments, the first sociologist provides the classic formulation of the approach and the second sociologist is a contemporary leader in that approach. Each explanation ends with some evaluative points that you could use in essays. However, you will also earn valuable AO2 marks by being able to compare and contrast the theories.

Argument 1: secularisation is occurring

The argument is that secularisation is occurring in modern industrial societies and that there is a good chance that, as developing countries industrialise, they will also experience secularisation.

Bryan Wilson: the significance of religion declines with modernisation

Bryan Wilson is seen by many as providing the first major theory of secularisation in the modern era. In 1966, he defined secularisation as 'a process whereby religious thinking, practice and institutions lose social significance'.

Bryan Wilson

What is meant by religious thinking, practice and institutions?

Task 4.3

If we use Wilson's definition we must decide the following:
- Which thoughts, practices and institutions are essentially religious?
- What might suggest a loss of social significance?

How would you answer these two questions?

In terms of religious thinking, Wilson (1976) examined primarily beliefs in God, heaven and hell. He took the view that statistics on these areas, which he viewed as overly optimistic, indicated decline and that religion was, therefore, less significant that it had been. He argued: 'Not only do fewer people believe, but everyone knows that fewer people believe and this very knowledge diminishes the credit of the church'. In terms of religious practices, he looked at membership and attendance figures and saw a decline. It was even the case in terms of the number of people seeking to train for the priesthood.

Religious institutions had a much reduced voice and impact when it came to decision making in a national and personal sense. This was partly due to the Roman Catholic Church and then the Church of England losing monopoly status because of various splits and schisms and partly due to the resulting indifference that people had towards religion. The outcome was a decline in the significance of religion; it no longer mattered to people and no longer commanded their respect. In Wilson's view, people were increasingly rational and wanted a natural rather than a supernatural explanation for events in their lives. He also argued that secularisation, via modernisation, affected the 'ancient creeds' of Judaism, Hinduism and Islam, as well as Christianity. Some sociologists had pointed to a growth of new religious movements as an example of vitality in religion. Wilson took the view that these new religious movements might initially appear attractive to people but that over time their appeal would wane.

He concluded that religion would not die out completely. It might well linger in private, although its public life does appear to be limited. This was enough to indicate secularisation, because religion would no longer have a significant impact on social life.

Evaluation of Wilson

- Aldridge notes that Wilson provides a 'powerful elaboration of the secularisation thesis', and that his concentration on the public and declining impact of religion on society in general is valuable. Aldridge feels it is an area missed by those who refer to privately held beliefs and commitments to support the idea that secularisation is not happening; these may be important but they do not have a major societal impact. He feels that religion might have brief revivals, which critics of Wilson would use to assert their opinions, but that the long-term trend is one of decline.
- Hamilton (2001) says that Wilson's contribution to the secularisation debate is seminal — it was the seed for much of the work that followed. Wilson sees science as a cause of secularisation, but Hamilton suggests that the growth of science and the decline of religion are two sides of the same modernisation process. One has not caused the other.
- Bruce supports Wilson's notion that secularisation has occurred. Even though religion still exists in the minds and actions of some people, what matters is that it is no longer so important in society in general. In fact, Bruce takes a good deal of his theory from the original work of Wilson, and it is to Bruce that we now look.

Steve Bruce: indifference to religion will increase

In 2002, Steve Bruce argued: 'I expect the proportion of people who are largely indifferent to religious ideas to increase and the seriously religious to become a small minority.'

Over recent years, Bruce has been seen by other sociologists to argue that secularisation and modernisation occur in tandem. His book *God is Dead* (2002) is an attempt to clarify his views. He says that his 'secularisation paradigm' is an explanation only of the Christian world since the Reformation. It is neither universal nor predictive of the future (as others had assumed it was). He goes on to temper this claim by saying:

> However, it does seem reasonable to see some social changes as accumulating in a 'value-added process'…once they have occurred, it is very difficult to see how their

effects can be reversed in any circumstances that are at all likely…We are claiming irreversibility, rather than inevitability.

S. Bruce, *God is Dead* (2002)

In other words, secularisation will not definitely happen, but he cannot think of any reasons why religion might become important again. He feels that many people are already indifferent to religion and that this indifference is only likely to grow. Like Wilson, he is arguing that religion has lost its social significance. The reasons for this are many and complex. They are summarised below.

Steve Bruce

Bruce's secularisation paradigm in conceptual outline: factors contributing to secularisation

- **Structural differentiation** This refers to the loss of functions by the major churches. In the past, areas such as education, health and welfare were the preserve of the church; now they fall under the remit of government control. Parsons (1965) thought that this was a positive thing, because churches could concentrate on their primary religious functions — explaining God's word and offering spiritual guidance. However, Bruce argues that it is evidence of secularisation, because the church is no longer as significant in the eyes of people as it once was. Where the church does still provide education or social care, Bruce argues it does so according to overridingly secular values.

- **Social differentiation** Economic modernisation of society has led to much social and geographical mobility. It has resulted in the fragmentation of communities and the ideas that they hold dear (including religious ones). In stable communities it is easier to adhere to core values. With modernisation, communities are changing; people encounter new ideas and new values. The church finds it difficult to argue 'one truth, one word', because its adherents face a range of alternative 'truths' from other sources.

- **The Protestant ethic** This commitment to work and self-discipline, noted by Weber, led to economic prosperity and modernisation, which led to structural and social differentiation.

- **Individualism** The Protestant Reformation — the break with Catholicism — led to a fragmented religious culture. Previously, the one church could claim authority on the truth, but the split (and subsequent breakaways from the Church of England by nonconformists) led to what sociologists call religious pluralism. This diluted the authority of the churches by creating 'a large number of competing perspectives and institutions', which gave individuals scope to follow their own truth. As a result, churches lost significance.

- **Societalisation** This term, drawn from Wilson, refers to the weakening of local communities as a result of their loss of power to national government when the nation-state became the central organising authority. The community has less to tie it together and fewer communal events to draw it together. The church would have played a central part in such events. When they no longer take place, the church loses significance.

- **Privatisation** Increasing differentiation and individualism encourages personal and private interpretations of religious belief and practice — privatisation. This is what Davie (1996) refers to as believing without belonging. Davie sees this as a good thing, because it involves people making positive religious choices. Bruce sees it as negative, undermining the social nature of religious worship that Durkheim (1912) thought was so important. It also means that there are no socialising bodies to pass on religious interpretations to the next generation. As a result, Bruce believes that religious orientation will die out.

- **Sects** Sociologists such as Stark, Fink and Bainbridge argue that the growth of sects is a positive thing for religion, because it indicates that people still have a strong desire for religious fulfilment, which the institutionalised churches are not offering. Bruce is highly critical of this position. He argues that sects add to the level of religious pluralism and that this further undermines the claims of churches (and the sects) to be authorities on religious truth. Like Neibuhr (1957), he argues that sects, over time, lose the vitality that encouraged people to join them and become like the institutions from which they drew members. Therefore, 'the sectarian project is largely self-defeating'.

- **Economic growth** Bruce notes how modernisation brings greater wealth to all and supports the argument of Inglehart (1997) that 'prosperity reduces religious fervour'. As noted in the earlier sections on Marxism, religion gives hope of a better life after death (e.g. heaven, rebirth). Poverty gives a reason for belief; wealth undermines this. Bruce feels that if people are having a good time now, there is less reason to invest religiously in a future beyond this life.

- **Science and technology** Bruce stresses that the impact of science and technology on religion is often misconceived. Some sociologists, he argues, have considered wrongly that secularisation results from science and technology, proving that God does not exist. Rather, he concentrates on the indirect impact that these disciplines had on religion by changing the way people ask questions about events and phenomena. It creates a 'general encouragement to a rationalistic orientation to the world' and 'increases our sense of mastery over our own fate'. As a result, religion is sidelined and people become indifferent to it.

- **Relativism** Relativism refers to the undermining of accepted universal truths — those things that everyone believes are true — in favour of the view that individuals have their own truths. Bruce argues that: 'Relativism is perhaps the most potent and most neglected part of the secularisation paradigm.' He suggests that relativistic positions have been taken up as a means of avoiding conflict between people or groups with different positions on the same topic — for example, on what counts as religious 'truth'. In a relativistic world, we can agree to differ on our interpretation of God and not fall out. For Bruce, this counts as secularisation, because it undermines the claims of churches to be the sole authorities on religious truth; in a relativistic world everyone is an authority on religion. This further reduces religious impact in society. He uses the example of interfaith marriage (e.g. between Protestant and Jew) to show relativism in action. In order for the marriage to work, the couple must put their marriage above religion, so religious faith is sidelined.

How is it possible to explain indicators of increased religiosity?

Bruce accepts that there are certain situations that retard the process of secularisation. These occur most obviously in two situations:

- **Cultural defence** When people are subject to rule by another country or ethnic group, or feel that loss of power is a possibility, religion provides a focus for expressing their ethnic or national identities. In a British context, this explains the heightened level of religiosity in Northern Ireland. It also explains high levels of religiosity in the former communist countries of eastern Europe and the Middle East.
- **Cultural transition** Religion helps people move from one culture to another by speaking the relevant language, sharing the same values and by providing contacts in the 'new' society. This explains the relatively high levels of religiosity among ethnic minorities in Britain. However, Bruce claims that this is likely to dissipate, as '...the third generation of Muslims is also approaching the English level of religious indifference'. Ethnicity and religiosity is further explored in Chapter 6.

Evaluation of Bruce

You need to decide whether Bruce is the adamant secularisation theorist that others see or whether, as he suggests, he is more measured in his claims. Certainly he feels that he has been unfairly criticised, although he accepts that his views are 'unusually pessimistic'.

- Woodhead (2001) argues that Bruce's view 'is now unusual and unfashionable'. Hervieu-Leger (2000) argues that he assumes a rather straightforward secularisation theory. She believes that trends in religiosity are more complex than Bruce suggests, with declines in some situations and increases in others.

- Misunderstandings might arise from the way that Bruce presents his theory. He claims to be talking about the decline in religion in the modern, essentially white, Christian world of Europe, USA and Australasia, but he appears to expand his theory beyond this. For example, he argues that 'across *the industrial world* [my italics] there is a steady and to-date unremitting decline in all religious indices'. Japan and Korea, for example, could be included in 'the industrial world', but these countries carry indices of high levels of religiosity.

- Some sociologists, for example Davie (2000), are critical of Bruce's attempts to apply the same theory to Europe and the USA. They see the USA as a religiously enthusiastic country, because it has indicators of high attendance and high belief. Bruce counters this by arguing that the high attendance comes from immigration and, therefore, represents cultural transition and that in any case the trends are downwards. He also believes that high-belief statistics come from people giving normative (expected) responses in surveys, rather than because they actually believe what they say.

- In support, Fenn says that Bruce is particularly helpful in pointing out that religion, rather than being a helpless victim in the secularisation process, has in fact been 'a major agent of secularisation', by rigidly arguing that only its view of the world is correct. This has led to religious pluralism and individual spirituality that has split religious consensus; 'the church has succeeded in destroying an ethos in which belief and practice were second nature…' (Fenn 2001). Fenn also accepts Bruce's assertion that religious belief has become more sporadic and occasional.

Argument 2: secularisation may not be occurring

The argument is that secularisation is not easy to define and that there is a good chance that it is not occurring.

David Martin: institutions expand and decline for various reasons

David Martin believes that religious institutions are no different from other institutions, in that they expand and decline for a variety of reasons.

Martin's classic study of secularisation was published in 1978. It built on earlier work and set the debate for those sociologists who were not convinced that secularisation was an inevitable consequence of modernity. He stated the case for saying that trends in religiosity (particularly attendance and membership) may be downwards at the time of his writing, but that the situation would not necessarily continue — religion could just as easily take an upturn in the future.

David Martin

When was the golden age of religion?

Some sociologists have attempted to pinpoint a golden age of religion (a time when religiosity was at its peak), in order to show that religiosity has subsequently declined. There were two variants of this 'golden age' thesis:

- The first golden age theory cited the Middle Ages as the high point of religion, because records suggested that almost everyone in Britain went to church. However, critics of this suggestion said that, although it may well be true that nearly everyone went to church, this was only because they were forced to by landlords who thought that it would help to keep the peasants under control.
- The second golden age theory claimed that Victorian society was the high point of religiosity in Britain, because attendance at church was not forced and Victorian society was very moral. Therefore, the word of God was lived as well as heard. However, critics argued that for many working-class people, attendance at church was a condition of their employment. If the workers did not go — to be indoctrinated — they would be sacked. For rich people, it was important to be seen at church; those who did not attend had lower status. Critics also rejected the idea that society was extremely moral — behind closed doors the Victorians were getting up to things that would make even people these days blush!

Martin (1969) was critical of the attempts to pinpoint the peak period of religion, because later changes would result in a conclusion of secularisation. He said that the story was not so simple. He argued that religious institutions expand and decline for various reasons, and that we should not assume that secularisation is occurring if some are in decline, because others could be rising to take their place, or people could be choosing to worship in their own way.

If there were to be a decline in religion, what conditions might lead to it?

Although he was critical of sociological arguments for the secularisation thesis, Martin was prepared to accept that certain historical and social conditions might lead to secularisation *in the short term*. He developed what he called a general theory of secularisation to explain this: 'The general theory is general in that it relates "universal processes", which are empirically quite well established, to a typology of cultural contexts.'

The general theory argued that religious practice declines with:
- heavy industry
- concentrated areas of working class people
- urbanisation
- geographical and social mobility

These features drew people away from church attendance, mostly because the church no longer had intimate knowledge of its adherents, as was the case when people lived in small rural communities. Populations were on the move, so the church could not make them feel guilty for non-attendance in the same ways as before. It could not keep track of who was in the area and who was not. Non-attendance was also due to lack of time and to the effect of Marxist politics, which were highly critical of religion among the working classes.

Such generalisations represented an ideal type for situations with everything being equal '...but things are not equal...The universal processes operate very differently according to the nature of that complex.' Martin argued that:
- Secularisation normally occurs within the bounds of Christian societies. Thus, a general theory can be stated for Christian societies and subsequently modified for other societies.
- Martin felt that the general theory was not announcing irreversible trends, but in some cases the trends might be 'quite limited'. For example, heavy industry, which he thought had a disastrous effect on religious attendance, was already in decline and, therefore, its influence on non-attendance would also decline. Trends could just as easily reverse with the new employment structures that took its place; the general process of secularisation may reverse.

There are many similarities here with the ideas of Bruce (2002). However, Martin is much more explicit about the short-term nature of these trends and more positive about the future of religion.

What could hinder secularisation?

Martin noted how culture affects religiosity. Looking at England he suggested: 'The English do not go to church very much, but they like to have it there. It is part of the legitimate order. It proves that God's in his heaven, and "all's right with the world". Belief varies in form and is spread widely, but religious practice is low.

Wales, Scotland and Northern Ireland, because of their remoteness, less industry and their national subcultures, are the 'bastions of majority religious practice' in the UK.

Martin, like Bruce (2002), noted a strong link between the growth of nationalism and the growth of religious attendance figures — what Bruce called 'cultural defence'. This was seen in the Soviet Union and Poland, prior to the breakdown of the communist regimes, as religion gave oppressed groups a way of channelling opposition to their communist rulers. The political differences in Northern Ireland also created high levels of religiosity.

Therefore, Martin (1978) concluded that: 'A general theory of secularisation such as I now propose need not assume that secularisation is a very long-term or inevitable trend.' Just as cultural trends had affected religious culture in these countries, they could impact in an alternative (but positive) way in other societies too.

Martin's recent work (2002) can be seen as an attempt to prove this. He has researched a great deal into the rise in Pentecostalism across the world, particularly in Latin America. He argues that it represents '…the largest global shift in the religious marketplace over the last 40 years', now involving about a quarter of a billion people worldwide, mostly in the developing world. Its success in Latin America allows sociologists to consider the secularisation process as 'historically temporary and geographically local'. However, he is also aware that this rise in Pentecostalism could follow previous Protestant models of initial rise followed by slump, such as occurred in Europe. Martin's preference is for the former argument, because he feels that this new Pentecostalism is well suited to postmodern conditions in the developing world. It is highly adaptable, so when adherents leave they tend to form new variants and draw in more people.

Evaluation of Martin

- Martin gains praise from commentators on both sides of the secularisation debate. Davie (1996), a keen supporter, feels that Martin has been able to reflect the complexity of the secularisation process. She has particular regard for his awareness of differences due to historical context and culture. She agrees that it is not a straightforward or linear process, and argues that close reading of his work is essential for all students of secularisation.
- Martin's fundamental conclusion is supported by Stark and Bainbridge (1987), who have become strong advocates for the idea that secularisation is a short-term, self-limiting process, because people will always need religion

to compensate for a lack of rewards in this life. They argue, as Martin did in the past, that secularisation is a myth. Martin wrote an essay in 1965 advocating that the word 'secularisation' should be removed from the sociologists' dictionary because it was so misused. Aldridge (2000) praises this claim for being 'intentionally provocative' and in opening up the secularisation debate.

- Bruce (1996), who sees progressive secularisation in Britain, is still able to argue that Martin has made 'some of the most important contributions to the (secularisation) paradigm'. Bruce sees his views as having much in common with Martin's *General Theory of Secularization* (1978), although Bruce feels that he is more pessimistic about the future of religion. Where Martin sees scope for new kinds of religiosity, Bruce sees Britain's religious culture as increasingly fragmented and secularised.

- Aldridge (2000) makes the point that Martin is an Anglican priest, as well as being a sociologist. This could leave him open to the accusation of subjectivity and being less forthright about the decline of religion than the evidence might suggest. However, even Bruce is ready to see Martin as an open-minded scholar.

Grace Davie: religiosity is evolving

Davie (1996) takes the view that religiosity is evolving; people are still religious, albeit in different ways than previously.

She is critical of claims that religious belief is dying out. She argues that religious life is 'mutating' and that 'the sacred undoubtedly persists and will continue to do so, but in a form that is quite different from those which have gone before'. Her

Grace Davie

The Pew Forum on Religion and Public Life

central theme is that British people have a tendency to believe without belonging. In other words, they believe in God and even in the truth of organised religion but, as a whole, they do not regularly participate. She agrees with secularisation theorists such as Wilson and Bruce that the statistical evidence for church membership and activity shows a decline. However, she feels that they miss the point that 'less conventional forms of religiosity have increased in the same period'. In some ways, the sacred becomes more, rather than less, prevalent.

European exceptionalism

Europeans exhibit what Davie (2002) calls unattached religion — most are not members of a particular church. However, at times of need (either physical or psychological), people go to churches for support and guidance. She calls this vicariousness — people expect that 'a minority [of clergy and attenders] maintain the [religious] tradition on behalf of the majority'. In this sense people see churches as public utilities (in the same way as they see water companies or hospitals), believing that churches should be there for everyone when they need them.

Davie is critical of western sociologists (e.g. Wilson and Bruce), whom she says have tended to focus on Christianity and then make generalisations to other religions worldwide. She feels that this is inappropriate — that it is dangerous to assume that what Europeans do today, others will follow tomorrow and that industrialisation always leads to secularisation. She believes that Europe is atypical and that the rest of the world operates on a different basis. Martin supports her in this claim.

Davie (2002) argues that 'believing' and 'belonging' are themes to help sociologists unpack the nature of religiosity. However, she is not keen to offer rigid definitions of the terms: 'Operationalising either or both variables is severely bound to distort the picture', resulting in arguments about the definitions, rather than examination of the developing trends in religiosity, which she feels is the more important role of sociologists.

Davie warns us that although the situation regarding religiosity is complex, it is possible to make a number of generalisations about religious belief (believing) and practice in churches (belonging) in contemporary Britain and beyond. The following list sums up her picture of varying levels of religiosity across the country.

Davie's suggested typology of belief, adapted from Davie (1996)

- In **inner cities**, belief is *depressed*. The inner city is characterised by a run down environment inhabited by poor, working-class people, who have a low record of church attendance. As a result, non-viable churches are closed. This further reduces religiosity in the area.
- In **city centres**, belief is *civic*. Cathedrals and large churches that are found in city centres become the focus of civic or public religion. They are 'the gathering place in moments of joy, danger, doubt or sorrow (the place of mourning after a disaster, for example)'. This represents a good example of vicariousness, a sense of 'We were happy for you to be there representing us in our absence, but now we have decided to come, make us feel better!'

- In the **suburbs**, belief is *articulated*. Suburbia, the richer edge of towns and cities, is characterised by articulate, middle-class individuals who actively choose the church they wish to belong to. They are keen to participate and to spread 'the word'. The churches of suburbia are 'flourishing…believing and belonging have come much closer together than is usually the case'.
- In the **countryside**, belief is *assumed*. People living in rural areas are good examples of believing and belonging *without* regular attendance. 'Local people assume that they are members of (the) church unless proved otherwise'. They prove it through attendance at social events (e.g. church fêtes), rather than by attending services.
- In the **Church of England**, belief is *uneven*. The emphasis is on declining practice and membership but 'certain parishes are still flourishing' (usually in middle-class areas). The Church of England is connected strongly with vicariousness.
- In the **Roman Catholic Church**, belief is *expressed*. 'The obligation of practice, of Mass attendance, is far stronger in the teaching of Catholicism than exhortations to practise are in Protestant teaching'. Therefore, believing and belonging are high.
- In **African-Caribbean churches**, belief is *communal*. Black Christian churches provide a range of welfare services, as well as religious ones. 'For many black congregations, the sense of community grows out of the church.'
- **Religious education** is about *traditional belief*. 'At the very least, religious education and **collective worship** have helped to keep in place some sort of religious culture, however tenuous this might be.'
- **Religious broadcasting** is an example of 'believing without belonging, *par excellence*'. Davie refers to this as 'the church of the air' and argues that audience figures and demand for religious broadcasting remain high. It allows religious involvement without leaving the house. It reinforces the messages of the main churches and provides stiff competition for 'members' at the same time.

Evaluation of Davie

- Davie is thought of highly by many sociologists of religion. Woodhead (2001) claims that Davie's work is 'more representative of current priorities in the field' than that of secularisation theorists such as Bruce, because she is looking for complexities of both secularisation and de-secularisation within the same society.
- However, in sociology one can have admirers (in this case, Berger) and critics (Bruce) at the same time. Bruce (2001) says that: 'Berger is much impressed by Grace Davie's (1996) thesis that the decline in participation in religious

institutions should not be taken as a decline in religious interest per se.' Berger summarises her work thus:

> What she found is that, despite the dramatic decline in church participation and expressed orthodox beliefs, a lively religious scene exists. Much of it is very loosely organised (for instance, in private gatherings of people) and has odd do-it-yourself characteristics…the presence of these phenomena casts doubt on any flat assertion to the effect that western Europe is secular territory.
>
> Berger, 'Protestantism and the Quest for Certainty', in *The Christian Century*, Vol. 26 (1998)

Bruce, however, is 'less impressed by the claims for "private gatherings" than is Berger. Attitudinal survey data show a steady fall in orthodox belief and even for such nebulous claims as a self-description as "religious"…' (2001).

- Bruce (2002) is critical of Davie on other grounds too. He considers her claim for 'believing without belonging' to be overestimated and, therefore, 'irrelevant'. According to Bruce, Davie and her supporters 'see it (spirituality/informal religion) a lot; I see little'. He believes that the weight of survey data suggests that people do not believe with either the strength or enthusiasm that they once did. The work of Davie and others who follow her line of argument is argued by Bruce to be 'methodologically inadequate'. Such sociologists, he asserts, have used 'vague and leading questions' and 'contestable cut-off points in sorting data', make false interpretations of data to suit their points and fail to tie their respondents down to concrete answers that would show their secularity.
- Bruce questions whether the private religious sentiments that Davie calls 'believing without belonging' can continue without a more formalised socialisation process to pass religious culture on to subsequent generations.
- Aldridge (2000) raises a similar point but is more open minded. He says that there is still evidence to suggest an interest by young people in religion, arguing that: 'Collective amnesia may be a threat but is not yet a reality.'

Task 4.4

An indicator of religiosity that Davie draws our attention to is belief in God, which is fundamental to virtually all religions. If people do not believe in God, there might be a strong argument for saying that secularisation is taking place (and that people neither believe nor belong).

Look at Table 4.1. What does it tell us? Could the evidence be argued to support Davie's notion of 'believing without belonging', or does it indicate Bruce's assertion that secularisation is taking place? If you accept Davie's conclusion, is the present level of religious belief likely to have a socially significant outcome?

Chapter 4

Table 4.1 Belief in God

Statement	Repondents (%)
I know God really exists and I have no doubt about it	21
While I have doubts, I feel that I do believe in God	23
I find myself believing in God some of the time, but not at others	14
I don't believe in a personal God, but I do believe in a Higher Power of some kind	14
I don't know whether there is a God and I don't believe there is any way to find out	15
I don't believe in God	10
Not answered	3

Source: *The British Social Attitudes Survey*, 1998 (www.statistics.gov.uk)

Task 4.5

Look at the following photographs of old churches. What do they appear to suggest, and which sociologists would make use of them to support their theories?

(a) Night club   (b) Furniture shop   (c) Church for sale

Clearly, the photographs in Task 4.5 indicate that churches are being sold for uses other than religion. This could suggest that people no longer wish to attend, but it may not give us an accurate picture of their religiosity. For example, there are not many people saying that selling off village pubs and post offices indicates that people no longer want to drink or to buy stamps. They just

70   Advanced **Topic*Master***

purchase these goods in different ways. Could it be that people attend in fewer numbers but gain religious and spiritual support in other ways?

Bruce (2002) argues that by about 2031 the Methodist church will have lost so many members that it will cease to exist. By then, the Church of England will also be quite insignificant. He asks whether his critics will then recognise that 'decline is not a sociological myth'.

You cannot afford to wait until then for a categorical answer, so you will need to decide now. What do you think of the concept of secularisation and why? Reading Chapters 5 and 6 will help you come to a decision, because much of the material relates to whether religion is declining or rising in popularity.

Summary

- Secularisation is a hotly debated concept.
- Part of the debate is over the operationalisation of the concept of religion; it affects the conclusions you make.
- The core of the debate rages over the indices of religiosity that are needed to measure secularisation.
- Advocates of secularisation, such as Wilson and Bruce, argue that all the major indices suggest a declining interest in religion and that, as a result, religion has less impact on society than it used to have.
- Critics of the secularisation thesis, such as Martin and Davie, argue that religion is changing. People are still privately religious and still prepared to turn to formal institutions when they feel the need. If secularisation is occurring, it is limited to western Europe.

Task 4.6

Assess the view that religion no longer plays a significant part in society.

Guidance

This is structured like a typical AQA question and, therefore, requires a range of skills.

- You need to show breadth of knowledge and understanding by referring to the two main arguments about secularisation.
- Build in assessment by looking at the strengths and weaknesses of both arguments and by showing how a definition of secularisation impacts on the research evidence selected for study.
- Plan the whole essay before you begin writing so that you can interweave knowledge and evaluation points throughout.

Task 4.6 continued

Explain the two major arguments:

- Secularisation is happening and religion is no longer significant (Wilson and Bruce).
- Secularisation is not happening and religion is evolving (Martin and Davie).
  Remember that the second argument is based on the view that people have great respect for religion and turn to it regularly, but privately, when they need it, and to the church publicly at important times in their lives.

The evaluative element should consider the strengths and weaknesses of both approaches. There will be much to gain by comparing the two main arguments directly.

The essay should conclude by summing up your assessment of the strengths and weaknesses of each argument. Is it enough to say that people do not go to church, do not think about the messages of the church and that religion has little impact on society? Or is it fair to say the people are spiritual in a new and private sense, and that this has a significant impact on society through their combined actions? Examples of this could be involvement in charity campaigns, in anti-war demonstrations, ethical buying and making ecologically friendly decisions. Do you think that people still have a respect for organised religion and are ready to turn to it in times of crisis?

Research suggestions

- Questionnaires or interviews about people's religious beliefs, opinions and practices will give you a good picture of whether secularisation is taking place and allow you to test the four main theories. Do people believe in God or heaven? Do they respect the church and other people's religiosity? Do they attend a place of worship regularly, occasionally or never? Which sociological argument is supported by your findings?
- If you feel confident, participant observation could allow you to experience why people attend a particular religious institution (and to hypothesise about why other people do not). From your observations, what do you think that churches do (if anything) to get more people through their doors? Make sure that you have the support of a parent or guardian before you do this.

Useful websites

- http://news.bbc.co.uk/1/hi/programmes/wtwtgod/default.stm
  This is a superb BBC site called 'What the world thinks about God'. It includes quizzes, detailed survey evidence and video excerpts. It is as close as you could get to the complete web support package.

- www.homestead.com/rouncefield/files/a_soc_rel_13.htm

  This site is designed for A-level sociology students. It offers a range of statistical data on the extent of religiosity in Britain. The other pages on the site that are about secularisation are also worth following up.

- www.tearfund.org

  This provides results of a 2007 survey on 'Churchgoing in the UK'. The report is made available as a download.

- www.christian-research.org.uk

  This site has up-to-date statistics.

Further reading

- Bruce, S. (2002) *God is Dead*, Blackwell.

  Chapter 1 provides a useful overview of Bruce's theory.

- Haralambos, M. et al. (2004) *Sociology: Themes and Perspectives* (6th edn), Collins.

  Pages 437–441 contain a range of statistical tables of trends in religiosity.

The changing structure of religion in society

Why consider the structure of religions?

This chapter looks at which religious organisations are in the fast lane, which ones are coming to a grinding halt, and why these changes are taking place.

Sociologists see religion fundamentally as having a social function. For this reason, some have spent a great deal of time trying to explain how religions are organised. Such research might provide information about why people start religions and also give an indication of their functions. It can provide information about how religions develop and give an understanding of how they respond to secularising forces. As a result,

tez@terryburton.co.uk

The Jesus Army has a contemporary appearance with its brightly coloured minibuses; its success is partly due to services that combine traditional religion with modern-day marketing, and music and dancing

sociologists may gain an insight into the future of religion. If religious organisations do not gain public approval, then they will fail and religion might die.

This chapter also considers the possibility that people want a less structured, more informal, kind of religion, and examines whether this means that religion has a significant future. It is possible that religion will be organised differently in the future, while still meeting the needs of society.

How are religions structured?

In order to decide how a religion is structured, sociologists have tended to look at:

- its hierarchy
- the membership and what is expected from it
- its relationships with the wider society

Early work was carried out by Max Weber (1864–1920) and developed by his pupil, Ernst Troeltsch (1865–1923). They set about forming typologies that would give a theoretical picture of religious organisation in an ideal situation. This was rather simplistic, but it gave other sociologists undertaking more detailed studies a chance to see how far their subject differed from the ideal. The work of Weber and Troeltsch is still used by modern sociologists as a starting point for discussion of religious organisations. According to Weber and Troeltsch, the key distinctions were between churches and sects:

- Churches were seen to be large-scale, national or international organisations (e.g. the Roman Catholic Church) and national state organisations (e.g. the Church of England). These were argued to be accepting of the social order, to reflect dominant group interests, to be dominated by members of the established elite and, although membership is open to all classes, to be overwhelmingly against social change.
- Sects were smaller scale and more active. Their members were often disaffected with society and wanted to be more involved in their religion. Weber felt that successful sects would grow into churches, just as Christianity had done. This would depend a great deal on the charisma of the leader(s). An example of an early sect is the Anabaptists; they challenged the authority of the established church.

In 1929, Niebuhr (1957) added denominations to the typology. He argued that denominations were sects that had lasted into a second generation. As a result, they had to develop a structure for socialising the children born to their members and for disseminating information to a larger group of people. This led them to lose their vitality and to become more mainstream — more like a church. They compromised with the secular world and their class base was predominantly middle class. An example of a denomination is Methodism.

The findings of these classical theorists are summarised in Table 5.1. It is simplistic, but contains the general principles.

An overview of the sect, denomination and classical church typology

Characteristic	Sect	Denomination	Church
Attitude to wider society	Rejects values and way of life	Compromise: no attempt to dominate society	Seeks to dominate the whole of society
Attitude of wider society	Ostracised	Either fashionable or neglected	Fashionable
Attitude to other religious groups	Intolerant	Tolerant	Intolerant
Attitude to members	Ideological and social domination of members	Ideological and social influence of members	Concentrates on domination of the world, not of members
Type of membership	Voluntary	Voluntary	Usually by birth; obligatory, therefore large
Basis of membership	Experiential and exclusive	Loose formal membership requirements	No membership requirements other than ritualistic
Social background of membership	Typically the economically deprived	Middle class	All inclusive, but leaders are wealthy and powerful
Scope	Local	National or international	National or international
Internal organisation	Often charismatic	Bureaucratic	Bureaucratic

Adapted from: G. Hurd et al., *Human Societies: An introduction to Sociology* (1980)

Task 5.1

There are several criticisms that can be made of this typology. Can you think of any?

Evaluation of the church–denomination–sect typology

A major criticism of the church–denomination–sect typology is that it is ethnocentric — it is too concerned with the Christian world and how religions are organised within it. It does not really account for the organisation of religions in the rest of the world.

However, there are arguments about whether it applies to the Christian world. Robertson (1970) argued that not all second-generation sects become denominations; some remain as sects. He called these established sects. A good example of this is the Quakers (also called the Religious Society of Friends).

Aldridge (2000) feels that Neibuhr was wrong in asserting that a second generation leads a sect to lose its dynamism. He offers the Jehovah's Witnesses as an example of a sect that has remained true to its core values despite large growth in membership. He argues that:

> The church–sect dichotomy has been a powerful tool of analysis. It is nevertheless limited in its field of application historically and culturally. The contrast of church and sect is characteristically Christian, with some parallels but no exact equivalents in other traditions.
>
> Aldridge, *Religion in the Contemporary World* (2000)

Aldridge goes on to argue that 'it applies to an age in which churches embraced the national population and enjoyed wide-ranging privileges granted by the state'. However, as indicated in Chapter 4, church membership is in decline. We need to consider the effects of this on religious organisations in general. Who are the winners and losers and what do our answers indicate about the future of religion?

Wallis (1976) developed a new typology that added cults to the structures of religious organisations. He maintained that cults are smaller than sects and, in general, make fewer demands on their members, who can drift in and out of membership. They are not necessarily religious in a substantive sense, but fulfil many of the functions of a religion. Like sects, cults have been seen as deviant by society. However, whereas some sects have attained a level of acceptability, cults may be thought of as dangerous because their members are perceived (perhaps wrongly) to be under the spell of a dangerous but charismatic leader.

An example of this is the Branch Davidian cult of Waco, Texas. This cult, founded in 1929, ended in the mass suicide/murder of 74 people, following a 51-day siege by the FBI in 1993. Its leader was David Koresh, a white, charismatic man, who believed he was the Messiah. Among other things, this belief arose because, in 1993, he was 33, and he was the son of a carpenter, as Jesus had been. He argued that he was prepared to lay down his life to save the world and that his followers should be prepared to do the same. The group had broken away from the evangelical Seventh-day Adventist Church, which itself is based on looking forward to the second coming of Christ. The apocalyptic end came after a dispute with the American authorities. Conspiracies abound as to whether the deaths were caused directly by the US authorities rather than being suicide.

Stark and Bainbridge (1979) argue that unlike sects, which often develop out of a break from a pre-existing religion, cults offer something entirely new. Importantly, there appears to be more disagreement than agreement about the exact nature of a cult. In general, it can be said that although it has

Flames engulf the Branch Davidian compound in Waco, Texas following a 51-day siege by the FBI

its faults, the classical typology does help us in analysing changing patterns of religious structures and organisations. The following sections attempt to see how far this is true by considering applications of the typology to modern examples.

Do modern-day churches match the typology?

Yinger (1970) felt that there was not only one kind of church. He distinguished between the universal church, such as the Roman Catholic Church, which is found across the world and the 'ecclesia', which tend to be churches based in a particular society (such as the Church of England). Stark (1967) argued that the latter were more likely to be associated with, and to compromise with, secular governments; both support each other. Evidence for this could be the physical and psychological link between the Church of England and the state:

- Lambeth Palace, the home of the Archbishop of Canterbury (who is selected on behalf of the monarch by the Prime Minister, from a shortlist of two) is situated across the Thames from the Houses of Parliament.
- The ceremonial church of the Church of England, Westminster Abbey, is across the road from parliament.
- The Archbishop of Canterbury and the senior bishops of the Church of England have seats in the House of Lords.

The church–denomination–sect typology suggests that the Church and state are closely linked. However, Bruce (1996) argues that the relationship is now much more fragmented. Growing secularisation and religious pluralism in England mean that the Anglican Church now has to compete with other religious groups for political favour. This may explain why, in recent years, the Church of England has been more ready to criticise government policy. For example, the church's report *Faith in the City* (1985) was critical of the then Conservative government's policy on poverty in urban areas. Other churches had done this previously, but Davie (1996) argues that because the criticism (which she says was relatively mild) came from the Church of England, it created much more of a political storm.

The typology suggests that churches are bureaucratic. In other words, they have a hierarchical structure for decision making and a set of paid officials to ensure they keep running smoothly. Bruce (1996) recognises such a structure in the Church of England: 'At the top is God, who talks to the archbishop, who talks to the bishop…who talks to the dean, who talks to the clergy, who tell lay people what to believe and do.'

Therefore, there is a top–down bureaucratic model in which messages pass in one direction only. Davie (1996) agrees that the Church of England has become more bureaucratic. However, the Church itself claims to be more democratic and sees information flowing up from the members as well as down from its leadership. It would point to the structure of synodical government that was established in 1970. The synod is a decision-making body for the church. It is divided into three 'houses' — the bishops, the clergy and the laity. It allows dioceses and parishes to send items for discussion and parishioners to be involved in that discussion, which means that what the church says will more accurately reflect the will of its members. This goes against the church–denomination–sect typology. Davie (1996) argues that this structure has actually made the Church of England more bureaucratic and that involvement in the synod requires a certain type of political personality that does not necessarily reflect ordinary churchgoers. She says this is likely to compound the bureaucratic nature of the church, but nevertheless feels that the synod has been a move in the right direction.

The Church of England website (www.cofe.anglican.org) argues that 'the church plays a vital role in the life of the nation'. However, Bruce believes that its loss of social significance and its falling attendances mean that it is now exhibiting qualities of a denomination. If this is the case, recent stories of church responses to declining attendances should be less surprising. They have included the use of an Elvis Presley impersonator in Truro

Cameracraft Photography

An Elvis impersonator who performed gospel songs against the backdrop of Truro Cathedral; churches are having to allow for the requirements of different congregations in order to combat declining attendances

Cathedral singing gospel songs and the creation of karaoke machines with hymns in different styles to allow for the requirements of different congregations.

Another response to secularising forces has been ecumenism — a joining together with other religions, Christian and otherwise, to offer central messages about God and morality. The Church of England is a member of the World Council of Churches and other ecumenical organisations. The church–denomination–sect typology presumes that a 'church' is intolerant of other religious groups. This is clearly no longer the case. The webpage of the World Council of Churches (www.wcc-coe.org/wcc/who/mch-e.html) gives an overview of the 342 Christian churches that belong to this ecumenical commitment.

Perhaps a more important sociological response to declining membership of, in particular, the Church of England, has been the Alpha course. In parishes that have tried it, it claims to have led to flourishing congregations. Alpha tries to encourage people to become practising Christians in a more relaxed setting, often making use of easy chairs (rather than wooden pews), and providing food and entertainment. The most important part is the dialogue that develops. So whereas the church–denomination–sect typology assumes that churches do not expect members to participate in any formal way, Alpha suggests that churches may have been like this in the past, but that they cannot afford to continue in this way if they want to survive. Alpha's website (http://alpha.org) claims that 8 million people have now attended an Alpha course. Grace Davie sees it as a significant development in the organisation of religion:

An Alpha evening meal conveys an informal atmosphere — entertainment is often provided

> The evangelical success story is epitomised in the Alpha course — a formula for welcoming those unfamiliar with the Church, which brings together biblical teaching, warm friendship and an emphasis on the Holy Spirit. The popularity of this movement is truly extraordinary — a fact admitted by friend and foe alike. Whether you like Alpha or not, it is hard to think of an equivalent (religious or secular) of parallel proportions.

Task 5.2

Using the website references provided above for further information, decide whether churches still fit the generalisations made in the classical church–denomination–sect typology. How far have modern churches adapted to fit new circumstances?

Do modern-day denominations match the typology?

The church–denomination–sect typology views the denomination as a compromising organisation in terms of its own members, other religious groups and the outside world. Hamilton supports this notion:

The denomination…has only formal procedures for admission and rarely any procedures for expulsion. It has a less distinct sense of self-awareness and is less exclusive [than a sect]. It admits to being one valid religious movement among others and makes no claim to exclusive possession of the truth. It is not separated from the wider society and its teachings and practices are less distinctive. It has a professional ministry and is not unduly antagonistic to prevailing orthodoxy.

Hamilton, *The Sociology of Religion: Theoretical and Comparative Perspectives* (2001)

Methodism is often quoted as being a good example of a denomination. It was formed by a preacher called John Wesley in 1739. Wesley stated: 'The world is my parish', by which he meant that he was willing to travel wherever necessary to pass on the word of God. He was famed for his travels around the country. Methodism began as a method of charismatic preaching within the Church of England. However, its alternative methods upset Anglican bishops and Methodists were increasingly banned from mainstream churches.

Although Wesley was educated at a top public school, Charterhouse, and at Oxford University, he and his followers were particularly successful in attracting the new industrial working class to convert. Bruce (1996) commented that: 'Like all "religions of the oppressed" the new Puritanism of the Methodists offered a comforting critique of the upper classes.'

Starting small, Methodism exhibited many sect-like qualities — it was zealous, experimental and appealed to the deprived. However, as the number of members grew it required a bureaucracy to serve them. Enthusiasm was lost, in favour of long-term security. Initially, members were required to conform to strict regulations, such as not drinking or gambling. However, as time has gone on, such actions have been left to 'personal morality'. These features match Niebuhr's prediction that if a sect lasts it becomes a denomination.

The Methodist website (www.methodist.org.uk) states that two-thirds of all Methodist services are led by local lay preachers, rather than by ordained ministers. The idea is that 'ordinary' Christians are just as capable of interpreting the word of God. Therefore, this Church should be more democratic than the established Church of England. It has many representative bodies (including youth and women's networks) at local, regional and national level, but also has a series of offices to deal with specific issues affecting the Church. This matches the typology, in that Methodism is ready to respond to its members, but also has a bureaucracy.

Like the Church of England, Methodism is having to deal with falling membership. Bruce (2002) claims that this issue is particularly important for the Methodists, because most members are old and they are not gaining enough new members to replace those who die. Sawkins (1998) reveals that: 'Apart from…one year (1985), every year since 1957 has shown a net decline, usually of between 2 and 3%. If that remarkably consistent trend continues…the Methodist Church will cease to exist in 2031.' The Church, he claims, has compromised so much with the world and its members that it has nothing left to offer.

The Methodist Church has responded to this by developing a policy for its clergy, youth workers and laity for working with children and developing their commitment to Christ. It reminds Methodists that all children should be welcomed into the church and that a church that does not do so will suffer. Given Sawkins's prediction, children are clearly essential to the future of the church. However, Methodists would also claim that children have always been uppermost in their minds. For example, Methodists were the founders of NCH (National Children's Homes) in 1869. The website www.methodistchildren.org.uk focuses on work with young people. It claims that 25% of Methodists are children. However, it is one thing for parents to take their children with them to church, but it is another for the church to convince them to stay on when they are capable of making their own decisions. The Methodist commitment to hearing children's opinions locally and nationally will help. This information suggests that Methodism is a denomination because it allows participation by all its members, even young people.

Do modern-day sects match the typology?

Hamilton (2001) claims that discussions of the church–denomination–sect typology have become 'somewhat tedious and sterile', but argues that studies of sects have proved to be more interesting. For him, sects are ' something of a laboratory for the sociologist of religion', because:

- they can be researched from the beginning of their existence, telling us something about how a religion starts and grows
- most of their members are recent converts, so sociologists can find out what inspires people to be religious

These are clearly key issues; the central debate for us, however, is how far modern sects meet the characteristics of the classic typology. Some sociologists refer to sects as new religious movements, because so many have been established since the 1960s. Others argue that 'new religious movement' is a misnomer because many of the sects referred to as 'new' have been established for many years (e.g. the Salvation Army and the Quakers). It is only that sects have become more visible since the Second World War; they are not significant in terms of membership numbers. Some have only a dubious religious quality; much of their description as 'religious' depends on the definition of religion used. Wilson (1999) adds that new religious movements can be worldwide movements, which we would not expect from the typology, and that they differ significantly from it. No comparison can be made with the past, because modern new religious movements are more diverse and draw from a much wider spectrum of religious traditions.

Wilson (1976) suggests that sects have the following characteristics:

- They are voluntary associations that people choose to join.
- Membership is by proof of special merit, such as knowledge of holy teachings.
- Exclusivity is emphasised and expulsion of deviants is exercised.
- Members see themselves as special because they share a unique view of the world.
- The emphasis is on the laity, rather than clergy.
- Members are expected to aim for personal perfection and to meet clearly defined requirements.
- Through the use of rules, sects have a totalitarian (or authoritarian) hold over their members and their ideology is used to keep members apart from society.
- They are indifferent or hostile to the secular society and the state.

Task 5.3

Compare Wilson's typology with the classic typology for sects in Table 5.1. How far is it similar or different?

Wallis's research (1976) has focused on the Church of Scientology, formed by L. Ron Hubbard. Wallis argues that it did not begin as a sect, but as a 'therapeutic system'. Its sectarian character emerged relatively late when the therapeutic method — know as Dianetics® — was seen to have religious implications. Dianetics® was a form of psychotherapy that directed people to think back to childhood memories in order to eradicate hurtful experiences from the unconscious. It became Scientology when a theory of reincarnation was added — the thetan. The aim of practising Scientologists is to obtain a state of 'clear' or 'operating' thetan. The thetan is the 'true self' of each individual, which has existed since the beginning of matter, energy, space and time. To reach a clear thetan (i.e. inner perfection/harmony), training is given through a series of stages/courses. The client must pay for this training, which is expensive. Recruits are not the traditionally dispossessed (as suggested by the church–

denomination–sect typology); they are mainly middle class. Some members are famous, such as the actors Tom Cruise and John Travolta.

Unlike most other religions, salvation is 'this-worldly' (i.e. it will happen now and will not leave the believer waiting for death in order to achieve it). It is achieved by the individual through a client relationship with the 'church', rather than as a collective or communal achievement (as with most other religions). Introductory sessions cost $750 and advanced sessions between $8000 and $9000. This has laid Scientology open to the claim that it exploits its members for financial gain. However, Scientology claims that it has to charge because it does not have the financial resources of more established churches.

Wallis suggests that the Church of Scientology might undergo a process of denominationalism, because it would come to compromise more with the wider society. He admits, however, that such an apparent compromise could be a public-relations exercise, designed to convey that image, while masking persistent sectarian aims. The Church of Scientology has attempted to become more respectable by being actively involved in programmes and campaigns for social reform and by emphasising its religious character and subduing its claims for therapeutic methods. The aim of this would be to protect the movement against further attack by society. Scientology has been the victim of various purges, court actions and enquiries by those suspicious of its aims and objectives.

The church–denomination–sect typology argues that sects are based on charismatic leadership. In other words, they are led by virtue of their leaders' strong personalities and their ability to persuade members to meet the requirements of the sects. Wallis tells us that Scientology's leader gained control over the Church through the development of his theory: 'The attitude of Hubbard's followers towards their leader justifies the description of him as charismatic. They see him as having access to supernatural knowledge of a kind never before revealed.' Scientology claims to have 10 million members which, if true, would call into question whether it is a sect or a denomination. However, claimed membership statistics can always be called into question, particularly when a sect wants greater respectability (as Scientology does). Reitman (2006) states

Task 5.4

Go to www.scientology.org (the official Church of Scientology website) and do one of their free personality tests. Be prepared for them to find faults with your personality, so that they can then offer you a 'course' in order to improve it. Decide if you feel this offers a religious insight and if Scientology is a sect.

that the Church of Scientology now owns 200 businesses in Clearwater (the headquarters of Scientology) and has schools and private tutoring programmes, day care centres and a drug rehab clinic. This suggests an increasingly bureaucratic organisation or, for the more sceptical, a business, rather than a religion.

Have there been any recent developments in British religion?

On page 75 we noted Troeltsch's contribution to the classic church–denomination–sect typology. In some ways it was simplistic, but Aldridge does praise him for his recognition that the 'mystical' would become an increasingly important force in society. In other words, people would become more concerned with individual experiences and place them at the forefront of religion. However, it would maintain an organisational structure, albeit much less formal and dogmatic than previously. Today, sociologists have developed this concern in the study of New Age religion. However, this tends to be individualistic and lack formal structure. What people do is rarely organised, being dependent on their own individual thoughts and actions. This brings into question whether the church–denomination–sect typology has relevance in the postmodern world.

Task 5.5

- Have you heard of any of the following: aromatherapy, astrology, earth mysteries, feng shui, herbalism, meditation, mysticism, tarot, Zen, homeopathy? If so, did you hear about these from books, magazines, CDs, lectures or friends?
- Do you (or your friends) buy any of the products linked to the above? If so, do you buy from an organisation that resembles a church, from a shop or stall or from an individual?
- How far do you believe the claims of the contents of such material? Are they life-changing for you or for others?
- Do New Age beliefs and practices seem religious to you?

New Age beliefs and practices have their roots in the late nineteenth century but became popular from the 1980s onwards. Bruce (1995) identifies four themes of the New Age:

- **New Science** Its emphasis is antagonistic towards western, authoritarian, positivistic and conventional science and medicine. Rather, it draws upon 'ancient', 'traditional', 'pre-modern' approaches — for example, aromatherapy, meditation and faith healing.

- **New Ecology** Its emphasis is on 'green' approaches and living with the environment rather than controlling it. 'The Secular Green protects the environment out of self interest; the New Age Green does so out of respect for a superior being' (Bruce). Emphasis is on the dawning of the Age of Aquarius, an astrological time characterised by creativity and spontaneity. Examples of the New Ecology include naturism and homeopathy.
- **New Psychology** and **New Spirituality** Like Scientology, these emphasise the potential of the perfect self within. The aim is to find it, draw on it and develop it. The psychological route draws on, for example, psychoanalysis; the spiritual route draws upon eastern religions, the belief in reincarnation and the search for nirvana.

Followers are more like consumers than believers. Personal contact, if any occurs, is likely to be through lectures or workshops. Different forms of New Age movement may tour together — for example, through 'psychic fairs' or 'mind, body and spirit conventions'. As a result, 'The notion of membership is redundant…Most of the movements are cults and even to call them movements is to imply a degree of cohesion and structure which they do not possess' (Bruce). He goes on to argue that a significant element of New Age is 'eclectic' — based on a combination of alternative beliefs and traditions. This leads people to acquire and absorb a range of beliefs and practices that they combine with their own culture. 'For some it is no more than reading a book and entertaining an idea; for others it is a change of world-view and direction comparable to conversion in more traditional religions.' Bruce's general view is that New Age religion is trivial and further evidence of secularisation. Its lack of organisational structure means that there is no socialising function, which would be necessary for beliefs and practices to be passed on to future generations in any genuine fashion.

Heelas and Woodhead (2001) are sociologists well known for their work on New Age movements. They take a more positive view than Bruce. Whereas Bruce views New Age religion as evidence of secularisation, Heelas and Woodhead see it as evidence of people looking for a spirituality that they cannot find elsewhere — mostly because existing institutions want to have authority over them, which they do not want. They believe New Age has a structure, albeit in a non-traditional form. New Age institutions are 'considerably less regulative and authoritative and therefore provide much greater freedom to exercise autonomy…with participants encouraged to express themselves, explore their feelings, grow individually and in relation to one another'. They go on to argue: 'The individual is not subordinated by the institution, but "is" the institution.'

Heelas and Woodhead note a huge growth in this area of religion as a result of people finding what they are looking for. Their study of Kendal (www.kendalproject.org.uk), a town in the Lake District with a population of 28 000, identified over 40 'new spiritual outlets' which support people in their personal religious quests. It is further supported by an array of 'virtual communities' on the internet. Blogging is helping individuals to share their religious experiences. They say that these all 'draw individuals together and make possible considerable cross-fertilisation of ideas, as well as face-to-face meetings and exchanges at weekends, workshops, conferences, festivals and so on'.

They argue that, taken together, their findings indicate that there is an institutional network that Bruce does not see; it does not, however, fit neatly into the classic church–denomination–sect typology.

Heelas and Woodhead see a spin-off from this, in that mainstream religions are also attempting to detraditionalise — to make themselves seem less authoritarian and more able to meet the needs of the individual. Alpha courses could be seen as an example of this; the Emerging Church network (www.emergingchurch.info) and the Alternative Worship (www.alternativeworship.org) could be seen as others.

Summary

- Traditionally, sociologists have defined a religious organisation as a church, denomination or sect.
- Sects are often referred to as new religious movements. They have been subject to much sociological research.
- The church–denomination–sect typology has increasingly been challenged for being ethnocentric and inaccurate.
- Case studies of the Church of England, Methodism and the Church of Scientology show that there is a degree of truth in the generality of the classic typology, but that individual religious organisations differ with regard to some characteristics.
- New Age religions challenge the classic typology by indicating that a new form of religiosity, without structure (at least in the traditional form), could be developing. This could indicate either growing secularisation or a new enthusiasm for religion.

Task 5.6

Assess the view that the traditional church–sect typology is no longer appropriate for the study of religion in the modern age.

Task 5.6 continued

Guidance

This is structured like a typical AQA question and, therefore, requires a range of skills. You need to:

- show breadth of knowledge and understanding by referring to the classical argument of Troeltsch and how it has been adapted by Neibuhr
- build in evaluation by looking at examples of modern religions, such as the Church of England, Methodism and the Church of Scientology; these will help you to decide whether the typology fits the organisational structures that it was designed for
- consider recent developments in religion that are less organised and formal — for example, the emerging church movement or New Age religion; these will help you decide whether the typology suits modern circumstances

Your conclusion should outline the world that the typology was designed to explain: one where the vast majority of people belonged to an organised religion of one sort or another. However, you will need to make a comparison with the world as it is now, where people are often not committed to any organised activity, particularly religion. In a religious world where secularisation is seen to be occurring, then it may be that religions will need to adapt to survive: less formality and less top-down instruction may be required. Your conclusion will need to decide how far this has already happened.

Research suggestion

Visit www.kendalproject.org.uk. This site outlines the study carried out by Heelas, Woodhead and others from Lancaster University. Click on to the page entitled *Research Opportunities for A-level Students*. It outlines specific interesting reading and research tasks. It invites you to send your results to Paul Heelas for inclusion in their wider study of 'The Spiritual Revolution' in the UK.

Useful websites

- www.religiousmovements.org
  This is the home site of the Center for the Study of Religious Movements at the University of Virginia, USA. It is a much-respected site that contains objective information about the Church of Scientology and other new religious movements. It also covers issues such as cult controversies, religious broadcasting and profiles of world religions.

- www.guardian.co.uk/religion/page/0,,818217,00.html
  This site is a useful reference for a range of religions in the UK, including the Church of England, Methodism and the Church of Scientology.
- www.bbc.co.uk/religion/religions/witnesses/organisation/
  Use this site to decide whether you feel that Jehovah's Witnesses are a sect or a denomination. This will give you another example to use in your essays.
- www.inform.ac
  This site was set up by Eileen Barker, who worked with the Unification Church (the Moonies). It provides objective information about new religious movements.
- http://news.bbc.co.uk/1/hi/programmes/wtwtgod/3517925.stm
  This is a BBC article on Alpha and the new charismatic churches.

Further reading

Blundell, J. and Griffiths, J. (2002) *Sociology Since 1995* (Vol. 1), Connect Publications.
This book has an excellent section on recent studies of religion, including the Kendal Project and research into New Age and neo-pagan movements. It includes interactive questions.

How far do social characteristics affect religiosity?

Social class

Mainstream Christianity

Social class has long interested sociologists because it appears to influence social behaviour. In the area of religion it seems to affect the level and type of religiosity exhibited by people. Chapter 4 showed that areas of Britain with high concentrations of the industrial working class were more likely to exhibit secular values, with church attendance being relatively low (Martin 1978). Martin suggested that, in part, this might be due to Marxist politics among the working classes, which argued that religion was used by the ruling class to pacify the workers, leading them to opt out.

Davie (1996), who agrees with Martin's key findings, indicates that in the inner city, where we would be most likely to find the poor working class, attendance has fallen so far that churches are being closed down. Davie also believes that:

- the middle class *either* exhibits religious belief and practice *or* neither. In other words, middle-class people are either strongly religious or irreligious; there is little middle ground. When middle-class people practise their religion, they tend to travel to a church that interests them and meets their needs, rather than attending their local church (even if it is a church linked to their religious affiliation).
- the working class show belief but not practice. They believe in God, but do not go to church (except for events such as baptisms, marriages and funerals). Even this practice has declined hugely since the 1960s.

Davie argues that the working-class pattern, once an exception, is now becoming the norm; British people 'believe without belonging'.

Martin's recent work (2002) on the growth of Pentecostalism argues that, on a global level, it is not so easy to characterise the middle class as religious and the working class as irreligious. In developing countries, both classes are equally likely to respond positively to enthusiastic evangelical Pentecostal churches, although they often attend at different locations. For the poor, the fairly strict rules offer some stability in a time of social and economic change. The wider support functions of the church (such as health, welfare and education) provide help for the working classes when it is needed. For the middle classes, Pentecostalism offers some respectability for their increasing wealth. It allows them to see it (as Weber argued Calvinists did) as a sign that God is pleased with them. However, Pentecostalism rarely extends beyond the emergent middle classes. This may well be due to the fact that the ruling elite is usually linked to more traditional religious variants because of their attachment to the higher levels of the state.

Outside mainstream Christianity

Social class can never be divorced from other social factors, for example ethnicity. However, it is possible to make some generalisations about social class and religion outside mainstream Christianity.

Islamic fundamentalism

Bruce (2002) notes a link between Islamic fundamentalism and the new socially mobile — those people who have experienced a rise from poverty and then found themselves unable to move any higher. This leads them to 'selectively imagine' the past. They remember (in part falsely) how close and supportive their communities had been and conclude that the fragmentation that they now suffer has been caused by western-sponsored modernity. They also 'forget' their past poverty and how much better off they are now. As such, we could argue that relative deprivation is more important than economic deprivation. People feel worse off in a variety of ways, blame the western, Christian, capitalist world for this and see Islamic fundamentalism as the answer. For Bruce, these outcomes apply to Islamic fundamentalists in Britain and abroad. However, Tibi (2005) suggests that Islamic fundamentalism arises among the poor, who blame the leaders' links with the west for their poverty. This feeling extends in the modern era as the mass media make them increasingly aware of their lack of wealth relative to people in the west — relative deprivation, but from a different dimension.

New religious movements

The classic church–denomination–sect typology (Chapter 5) suggests that:
- churches were predominantly for the ruling classes (and those who deferred to them), because of their links with the state

- denominations were for the middle classes because they offered positive reasons for their relative wealth and because they compromised with society
- sects were for the economically disadvantaged (the working classes), who were keen to change this world or to see the arrival of the next world, shared with God

Chapter 3 showed how millenarian movements were often supported by the poorest people in developing societies. They are often forerunners to working-class revolutionary political movements. Tired of waiting for change through God's arrival, they aim to change their lives in the present.

In modern times, the Jesus Army is seen as an example of a sect that aims its message at the economically disadvantaged, often targeting the poor and homeless. For this sect, this represents putting Jesus's words into action. However, critics say that it exploits the poor.

Task 6.1

- Go to www.jesus.org.uk to find out more about the Jesus Army; the 'people's stories, under 'J-Generation' are particularly useful.
- Then go to www.jesusarmywatch.org.uk/scrapbook/exmembers.htm, which offers a critical insight from some ex-members.
- Use the information gathered to explain why people might join the Jesus Army. Is it because of their social class or are other factors more important?

In the 1960s, the concept of relative deprivation was offered increasingly to explain people's participation in religion. It was argued that people who joined did so because they felt unfulfilled in some way. For example, Glock (1964) believed that people joined new religious movements because:

- they felt undervalued by those around them
- they had physical and/or mental health problems and, therefore, felt deprived
- they felt that other people were not meeting their high ethical standards and so felt deprived by living in a world that was not good enough for them
- they felt that they had a lack of meaning in their lives

Sects offered a sense of community with high ethical standards where people could find a sense of meaning. Research since then backs up these findings and helps to explain the higher number of middle-class people joining sects. Dawson (2003) supports the notion that new religious movements have drawn support from the relatively privileged and prosperous. He quotes Stark and

Bainbridge (1985), who state that new religious movements 'skim more of the cream of society than the dregs'.

Cynics argue that this is because there is money to be made out of middle-class joiners who are either socially inept or who have been brainwashed into membership. Dawson is critical of this argument and uses evidence from an in-depth study of joiners by Levine (2003) to suggest that they are primarily young people who have, in a sense, been smothered by their families and who are unable to develop their own identities. New religious movements offer them 'a way to separate from their families and explore their own nature, while remaining surrounded by a supportive and highly structured group' (Dawson 2003).

New Age religion

Bruce argued that New Age religion is popular with the more affluent.

> Spiritual growth appeals mainly to those people whose material needs have been satisfied. Unmarried mothers raising children on welfare tend to be too concerned with finding food, heat and light to be overly troubled by their inner lights and when they do look for release from their troubles they prefer the bright outer lights of bars and discotheques.
>
> S. Bruce, *Religion in the Modern World: From Cathedrals to Cults* (1996)

The middle class have money and found it has not necessarily proved to be everything. The working class have yet to find out. Those most interested in the New Age will be those in 'expressive professions' (e.g. actors and writers), whose education and work make them more interested in human potential.

Gender

Mainstream Christianity

Gender has been an important area of study in sociology for a number of years. However, until relatively recently this was not the case in the sociological analysis of religion. Bernice Martin (2001) and Linda Woodhead (2001) argue that study in this area has been gender blind.

Chapter 2 offers an explanation of feminist accounts of the function of religion in terms of the maintenance of patriarchy. There is much evidence to support this theoretical analysis. Puttick (2003) argues that the position of women in religion is paradoxical. They make up the majority of the 'consumers' of religion, yet they are seen as weak spiritually. In terms of roles in religion, they can be found 'arranging flowers on the altar, sweeping the temple floors, but not preaching or teaching'. If this were the case (and it could be argued that

Puttick oversimplifies the situation), then we might expect that men would be for religion and women would be against it. However, most evidence suggests that the opposite is true.

Bruce (1996) and Davie (1996) note how women make up the majority of Christian church groups in England, Northern Ireland and, particularly, in Scotland. This generalisation becomes even stronger when sociologists consider frequent churchgoers; the difference between male and female attendees is also increasing. Differences are greater still in terms of belief: more women believe in God, while more men are likely to disbelieve. Women and men also view God differently, with women concentrating 'more on the God of love, comfort and forgiveness than on the God of power, planning and control. Men it seems do the reverse' (Davie).

Why do women appear to be more religious than men? Davie feels that, because of their biology and their caring roles, women are much closer than men to birth and death. She argues that this encourages them to reflect more on the meaning of life (and death) and God's role in this. However, she accepts that 'the case is far from proven'. Woodhead (2001) suggests that women's greater religiosity is due, first, to the gendered division of labour, which has produced other forms of gendered activity — for example, religiosity. Second, it results from women viewing religion as compensation for their unequal position in society. She, like Davie, accepts the need for much more research to test these notions.

Although women are more religious than men, Woodhead notes that middle-aged women, in particular, are leaving the Church. She puts this down to changes in women's lives since the 1960s. Women's work, sense of worth and identities have changed, although not as much as they would have hoped. As women have begun to find patriarchy unacceptable in other areas of their life, they are also more likely to reject it in religion. This has led women to seek new forms of religion and spirituality. New Age religion has benefited.

Bernice Martin (2001) sees a different response to patriarchy in terms of global Christianity, particularly in the growing Pentecostal churches. Pentecostalism has provided a moral argument for men spending their leisure time with their families (rather than drinking or gambling). This means that men are likely to share a greater proportion of domestic tasks. However, there is a paradox here. Although this is happening, it has to remain unnoticed, because women cannot be seen to be exercising any power over men. It is also 'precarious', since women appear to gain more from these sets of relationships than men. As a result, men are more likely to fail to adhere to the church message than women. However, even when partners refuse to join their wives at services, women still gain from the community spirit and support that greets them in church.

Judaism and Islam

Swale (2000) reflected on differences between orthodox and more liberal interpretations of Judaism within the religion. The orthodox wing is the traditional, patriarchal version. It uses references from the Torah and Talmud (Jewish holy books) to suggest that women could distract men from religious thoughts, so they should not easily be visible in the synagogue. Their domestic duties should take priority over public worship. Such an argument has led to the separation by role and by space of men and women in the synagogue. Hence women, if they attend services at all, cannot participate fully, because they are either in a balcony or behind a screen.

Synagogue in St John's Wood, London; men sit on the ground floor, women in the gallery

Over time, Judaism (like Christianity) has seen many organisational splits. The liberal and reform movements have developed, which interpret the Torah in less patriarchal ways; some communities encourage women's participation in ceremonies. Some Jewish feminists, because they felt that patriarchy was too entrenched in Judaism, have developed new religious movements, creating new ceremonies to celebrate women.

Butler (1995) found similarities in her study of young Muslim women. Their religion was an important part of their identities and they still wanted to follow it, but they felt it had been interpreted by men to suit their own patriarchal needs. One woman said:

> Islam's not to blame for women being kept in the house, covered up 24 hours a day, it's the men folk that do this. It's not Islam, Islam doesn't impose and say you've got to do this…If your heart follows Islam then you follow Islam and clothing's got nothing to do with it, or culture. Cultures are man's invention, I suppose.
>
> Source: C. Butler, 'Religion and gender: young Muslim women in Britain', *Sociology Review*, Vol. 4, No. 3 (1995)

As a result of improved educational opportunities, women are better able to analyse the Koran and to challenge some of the restrictions arising from men's interpretations of it.

However, not all Muslim women feel this way. In June 2004, Shabina Begum, a 15-year-old student, went to the High Court to challenge her school's view that she should not wear the jilbab (clothing that covers the full body except the face and hands). The stereotypical view in the media (which is in line with some of the women in Butler's study) is that such dress — particularly the covering of the head — is about men asserting patriarchal control over women. This was the underlying message coming from Shabina's school, although the major argument was that such dress compromised health and safety rules. Having initially lost her case, Shabina argued successfully in the Appeal Court that it was her right as a Muslim woman to dress modestly in line with Islamic requirements. Muslim women in support of the veil argue that it gives them anonymity by helping them to avoid the male gaze. Academic work that backs up this point of view comes from Ahmed (1992), who argued that criticisms of the veil originate from European colonialists, including feminists, who wished to make Arabs more like themselves. She agrees that Islam, like other cultures, is patriarchal and that this does need to be challenged, but that the veil is not part of it. Arguments about the veil became pronounced in 2006 after former Home Secretary Jack Straw asked his female constituents in full veil to remove it before speaking to him.

Michael Stephens/PA/Empics

Shabina Begum

Task 6.2

(a) Go to http://speakingoffaith.publicradio.org/programs/muslimwomen/index.shtml. Click on Listen and hear Leila Ahmed speaking in favour of the veil for Muslim women. Imagine you had the capacity to phone-in a reply. What would you say? Would you be supportive of her arguments or critical of them? Why?

(b) Follow up the arguments on the veil made by Jack Straw and government ministers such as John Prescott and Phil Woolas in 2006 on sites such as http://news.bbc.co.uk/1/hi/uk_politics/5410472.stm and www.guardian.co.uk/religion/Story/0,,1889846,00.html. How far do they support the comments you made in answer to part **(a)**?

New religious movements

Puttick (2003) suggests that because most new religious movements are adaptations of world religions, they tend to reflect their patriarchal assumptions and practices. This is particularly true of those that stem from Christianity. However, she does feel that this has been less the case since the mid-1980s, putting this down to the influence of feminist movements. Historically, there have been concerns that young female recruits to new religious movements have been sexually exploited and abused after being taken in by charismatic male leaders.

An example of this was the Children of God sect, which required young female members to attract new male members by having sex with them.

Puttick (2003) argues that despite the obvious downsides for women, new religious movements offer stability and clear role expectations. They also 'offer women a range of options, from the traditional nuclear family to childless freedom'. Women can choose the movement that most suits their needs and attitudes. Some have given leadership options to women. Some women, such as Mary Baker Eddy (Christian Science), have founded sects. Research suggests that women leaders bring an emphasis on feminine traits such as 'practicality, intuition, tenderness, body affirmation, caring, healing, devotion and forgiveness…'.

Task 6.3

Find out about the life and theology of the founder of the Christian Science sect, Mary Baker Eddy. How was she able to convince women and also men to follow her, when most other religions have been led by men?

Age

Mainstream Christianity

Task 6.4

Examine the bar chart. What are the trends related to age and religion? Try to explain these.

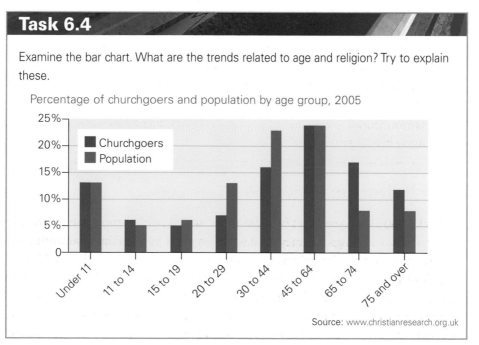

Percentage of churchgoers and population by age group, 2005

Source: www.christianresearch.org.uk

Davie (1996) concludes that: 'Older people have always been more religious than the young…It seems that belief in God, and specifically belief in a personal God, declines with every step down the age scale, as indeed do practice, prayer and moral conservatism.' However, this only reflects age groups where people are free to choose. Attendance (if not belief) statistics are higher for young people who are teenage or below, but this may be because of parental encouragement or compulsion rather than free will. Davie finds it significant that young people in their twenties are least likely to show religious behaviours because these are the people most likely to have children — if the parents are not religious, they are not likely to socialise their children for them to become religious.

Socialisation is important in determining children's understanding of religion, just as it is their understanding of other areas of social life. A key factor will be parental influence.

David Voas (2005), on www.manchester.ac.uk, stated that: 'How children are brought up has an enormous impact on whether they will identify with a religion. Once people become adults, their affiliation is less likely to be affected by influences around them.' Voas has found that:

- if a child has two religious parents there is a 50% chance of the child adopting the religion
- if a child has only one religious parent there is a 25% chance of that child adopting the religion
- if a child's parents are not religious they are unlikely to become religious

---

Box 6.1
Children's letters to God

- Dear God, did you mean for giraffes to look like that or was it just an accident? (Norma)
- Dear God, instead of letting people die and having to make new ones why don't you keep the ones you got now? (Jane)
- Dear God, I like the Lord's prayer best of all. Did you have to write it a lot or did you get it right the first time? I have to write everything I ever write over again. (Linda)
- Dear God, thank you for the baby brother but what I prayed for was a puppy. (Joyce)

TopFoto

S. Hample and E. Marshall, *Children's Letters to God* (1991)

Voas thinks that the failure of obvious religiosity to be passed on to the next generation contributes to increased secularisation within the UK, but Davie disagrees. As far as she is concerned, religious belief never totally disappears, although it may not necessarily be Christian in nature. It can be seen to emphasise morality and ethics, as well as an ecological concern for the future of the planet.

Parents are not the only influence on a child's religiosity; secondary socialisation by peers is also a factor. It is at school that children might develop friendships with those from other religions. However, faith-based schooling is likely to have minimal impact on children's religious beliefs.

Over recent years, moral socialisation has been a concern of both Conservative and Labour governments. Their assumption has been that secularised parents bring up children who lack morals and that this has resulted in a rising crime rate, because young people do not know right from wrong. For this reason, politicians have sought to increase young people's religious education in state schools in the hope of making school children more morally aware.

Task 6.5

Find out what governments have asked schools to do in terms of spiritual and moral education. Take a look at www.QCA.org.uk/downloads/6153_re_adult_life_spirit_moral_dev.pdf and summarise it into a list of key points. Then talk to a range of parents, teachers or lecturers about whether they think that it is the responsibility of a school to teach religion and morality. Of the arguments you hear:
- which do you most agree with and why?
- will they help to make children more moral?
- how do the ideas compare with the requirements of the government?

Islam

The debate about the impact of religious education becomes more controversial when the focus is on Islam. There has been widespread concern in the media that Islamic fundamentalism has spread through the indoctrination of young men in Islamic schools both in Britain and abroad, particularly in Pakistan. Terrorists such as the London bomber Shehzad Tanweer have allegedly been brainwashed in a Pakistani madrassa. Muslims say that madrassas teach about the Koran and often provide the only opportunity for children to be educated. They also provide other important welfare functions. Therefore, Muslims argue that madrassas can no more be blamed for turning Shehzad Tanweer into a terrorist than the British schools that educated him.

In response to demand from parents, there has been a growth of Islamic schools in Britain. In September 2003 there were 53; by January 2005 there were 118. They are mostly independent schools. David Bell, head of Ofsted at the time, argued that such schools were failing to prepare their students adequately for life in British society. This view upset the Muslim community in Britain, who believed that his arguments were overly sensational. In 2005, the Islamic Human Rights Commission (2005) stated that Islamic schools were preferred by 47.5% of Muslim parents because they were stricter, more moral and linked to religious values. However, the report also indicated that while 61.2% of 30–40-year-olds wanted such schools, only 37.8% of 15–19-year-olds wanted them (www.ihrc.org.uk/show.php?id=1409).

In response to all the arguments, the government has enabled Muslim communities to set up their own state-funded schools. This will allow the schools to be monitored more effectively so that possibilities for indoctrination are reduced. It also allows the government to reward non-fundamentalist Muslims by putting their education on the same footing as that of Christians who have long had state-funded schools. This policy has already had a major success: Feversham College, an all-girl Muslim secondary school in Bradford, came top of the national league table for value added progress in 2005.

New religious movements

Dawson (2003) argues that: 'The membership of most new religious movements is disproportionably young,' and 'relative to the population, middle-aged and old people are markedly underrepresented.'

- Barker's study of the Unification Church (Moonies) in 1984 found half its membership to be aged between 21 and 26.
- Rochford (1985) found over half the membership of the Krishna Consciousness movement to be between 20 and 25 years of age.
- Wilson and Dobbelaere (1994) found 68.2% of the membeship of the Buddhist Nichiren Shoshu movement to be under 34 and 88.4% to be under 40.

Dawson feels that such findings are particularly representative of movements that are demanding of their members. Balancing family and religious life proves to be too difficult, so middle-aged people leave. Those that are less demanding of their members, for example the Church of Scientology, are likely to have a wider age profile. The average age of people becoming Scientologists was found by Wallis (1976) to be 32.

Levine (2003) argues that new religious movements appeal to a specific type of young person — one who yearns for independence from a smothering family, but who lacks self-esteem and, consequently, the ability to break free. New religious movements offer a quick fix to their desire to break away from their parents and provide a supportive community that takes their place. This may explain why families assume that their children have been brainwashed. If the parents have not been conscious of being so restrictive, they will find it hard to understand why their child has left such a 'loving' family. However, Dawson warns us that much of the other evidence linking age distribution to new religious movements is largely speculative.

Ethnicity

Since the Second World War, ethnicity has played an increasingly important role in patterns of religiosity in Britain. The ending of colonialism during the postwar period has seen a range of ethnic groups coming to Britain, on the whole to fill gaps in the labour market. Religion has been an important part of the cultural identity of these immigrants, which is why Britain has seen the growth of a diverse pattern of religiosity. Table 6.1 shows recent census statistics on religiosity in this country.

Table 6.1 UK population, by religion, April 2001

Religious status	Thousands	%
Christian	42 079	71.6
Buddhist	152	0.3
Hindu	559	1.0
Jewish	267	0.5
Muslim	1 591	2.7
Sikh	336	0.6
Other religion	179	0.3
All religions	45 163	76.8
No religion	9 104	15.5
Not stated	4 289	7.3
All no religion/not stated*	13 626	23.2
Base	58 789	100.0

*Includes 234 000 cases in Northern Ireland, where data are only available as a combined category
Source: Census, April 2001, Office for National Statistics (ONS); Census, April 2001, General Register Office for Scotland (GROS)

Task 6.6

What are the major trends evident in Table 6.1? How might you explain these?

The majority of people claiming on the census to be Christian will be white indigenous Britons, but many will be of black African and black Caribbean descent. Others will be of European descent — for example, Irish, Polish, Italian, Greek and Croatian. Most Jews are also of European descent. They have a long history in Britain, having arrived at different historical periods, often to avoid persecution. British Muslims are mostly of Pakistani, Bangladeshi and Indian descent, but they are also from the Middle East, Turkey and, more recently, from Bosnia and east Africa. Hindus and Sikhs are predominantly of Indian descent. There is clearly a diverse spread of religious affiliation. Although families may have been settled in Britain for several generations, primary and secondary social-isation has ensured that religious beliefs and practices developed outside Britain have been passed on.

Herberg's study of migrants to America argued that religion offered them a mechanism for smoothly transferring from the home country to the new one. Each national group set up its own church, using its own language, even though the same religion might already be catered for in an English-speaking American church. This provided the opportunity to meet other people with similar char-acteristics, language and values. These people would have other contacts — this could lead to housing, employment and social networks, thus enabling migrants to ease themselves into the new culture. Therefore, Herberg argued that reli-giosity became of crucial importance for the new migrants:

> The church and religion were for parents the one element of real continuity between the old life and the new. It was for most of them a matter of deepest concern that their children remain true to the faith. In their anxiety, perhaps not only for their children but also for themselves, they tended to make their pattern more rigid than it had been before the great migration. 'What could be taken for granted at home had zealously to be fought for here.'
>
> W. Herberg, *Protestant-Catholic–Jew: An Essay in American Religious Sociology* (1983)

The children's response was either to adopt the religion wholeheartedly and become community leaders or to reject it in order to become 'American'. The grandchildren were likely to find a middle ground between the two extreme positions, explaining America's relatively high attendance at church.

As noted in Chapter 4, Bruce supports the application of Herberg's conclu-sions to Britain, noting how religion is used for 'cultural transition', which can make it *temporarily* significant. However, he believes that industrialisation and modernisation temper the enthusiasm for religion. In the long term, he believes, ethnic communities will become as secularised as the host community.

Herberg's study has important implications for the study of ethnicity and religion in Britain. Will we find a similar pattern of generational religiosity? Whatever the pattern, what are the implications for British society?

Mainstream Christianity

Bruce (1996) believes that the case of Irish immigrants shows the potential trajectory for the pattern of religiosity of other ethnic groups in Britain. Large numbers of Irish people settled in England and Scotland in the eighteenth and nineteenth centuries. Their religion, Roman Catholicism, served to draw together what were largely poor and dispossessed people. However, as they prospered through time, gaining better education, jobs and housing, the younger people began to find acceptance in the wider community. Previously, the new migrants had an expectation that their children would marry within their own religious and ethnic community. However, in gaining friends in the wider community, their children broke the expectation of marital endogamy. Rather than let religion create divisions within the new partnership, compromise between spouses led to religion having a less important role in their lives.

Task 6.7

What criticisms could be made of Bruce's argument that religion will become less important, in the long term, to ethnic minorities?

A major criticism of Bruce's arguments is that he overlooks a major difference between the Irish and some other ethnic minority groups — skin colour. People of Irish descent could find acceptance relatively quickly because they could pass for being indigenous British. Their children developed the same accent as their peers, wore the same clothes as their peers and, most importantly, looked like them. This is not true for people of Caribbean, African and Asian descent. Unless British society becomes more inclusive, the skin colour of these people will make it harder to be accepted. It could be argued that if they are not accepted in society, they will rely on each other for mutual support and religion will continue to play an important part in that support process.

At the present time, people of Caribbean and African descent illustrate the possible link between religiosity and lack of social acceptance. Their churches are booming. Christian Research (2006), led by Peter Brierley, argues that roughly three new churches have opened every week since 1998 and that approximately 50% have been to meet the needs of black and other ethnic minorities. Is this due to lack of social acceptance? Is it because their churches are more exciting? Is it because black people are more spiritual? The answer is not clear.

Robert Beckford (2004) argues that black evangelical Christianity poses a threat to traditional Anglicanism. While Church of England congregations are becoming increasingly old, black evangelical churches straddle the full age range and are booming. In inner London, 44% of churchgoers are black (www.christian-research.org.uk). He argues that this new black evangelicalism has been exported from Nigeria, where, he claims, some churches regularly have congregations of 100 000 at one service. Beckford suggests that the excitement generated by such an attendance and the upbeat delivery of a service gives these black Christians a greater sense of independence:

Robert Beckford

> Going to church taught me two things: that there was a higher power than myself and that blackness was something you could love, because every Sunday morning we would shout, sing, shake our bodies and celebrate being created in the image of God…Even to this day there is no other safer space for being black than black church life. Wherever you find black churches you will find kids going to university, people getting married, getting involved in business…It is still the hub of African-Caribbean life, offering hope and a prophetic vision of how things can be better.
>
> Robert Beckford, www.newnation.co.uk/iframe_story.asp?NID=1761

Homer Sykes/Alamy

A black Pentecostal church congregation

Beckford finds a supreme irony in the fact that white British Christian groups such as Alpha are learning their methods of evangelism from black African Christians. In Victorian times, white missionaries had gone to Africa to spread the word of God; now Africans here are doing the same. Beckford and Bruce agree that black Christianity represents an attempt by disenfranchised people to gain control over their own lives and to help them gain wealth. Black Pentecostalism often preaches that wealth can be a good thing — something to aspire to. This was illustrated in Pryce's study of the black community in Bristol (1979). He called the black Pentecostalists there 'the saints'. Their community offered the support of friends and provided a strict moral code that would help them gain wealth. Pentecostalism promoted the Calvinistic emphasis on work ethic and avoidance of acts such as drinking, gambling and dancing that might get in the way of a commitment to hard work. It also promoted the value of family life, guarding against increased poverty that could arise from family break-up.

Non-Christian ethnic minorities

Bruce (1995) argues that generalisations about Muslim and Hindu religiosity in Britain are difficult to make, because there are so many differences within each group. Muslims are split along theological lines between Shias and Sunnis; most British Muslims are Sunnis. Within each theological tradition there are further splits (similar to the widely differing interpretations within Christianity). Further splits result from differences in class, wealth and education, and whether the people had rural or urban origins in their 'homeland'. Hindus are similarly split. In Hinduism, this is further reinforced by aspects of caste — a hereditary notion of class and purity. Whereas splits between British Muslims are often too great to be overcome through shared worship, Hindus are more likely to come together in their temples.

Samad (2006) notes that British Muslims are characteristically younger than their white counterparts: 'Over 33% of British Muslims are aged up to 15 years of age and half are under 25'. This has important implications for the future of Islam in Britain. Bruce (2002) argues that young people of Muslim descent are likely to become more secularised: 'As they become English in every other respect, the third generation of Muslims is also approaching the English level of religious indifference.' Concern has been expressed about increasing fundamentalism among some young Muslims. However, Samad argues that there is no evidence of young working-class Muslims being more religious or more familiar with Islam than their parents — many are actually more secular.

This view can be disputed with reference to the work of Jacobson (1998). She looked at religion and identity among young British Pakistanis. Her view was that Islam continued to be an important part of their identities and that they were not being secularised. Islam provided young people with a certainty that they were unable to find in other areas of their lives. Their commitment to Islam was evident in how they lived their lives. Although they had non-Muslim peers and wanted to study, socialise and work outside the Muslim community, they were keen to maintain a psychological distance. They did this in a variety of ways, from formal practices such as attending a mosque or observing Ramadan to more informal ways, such as avoiding behaviour that would conflict with the teaching of the Koran (e.g. dating and drinking).

Samad notes a class difference in young Islamic identities. Poorer Muslims are likely to lose contact with their parents' language of origin and adopt English instead. Islam becomes rather more important to them as a condition of their identity. Middle-class Muslims are more likely to use their parents' language of origin as well as English. This gives them a stronger connection to their parents' country of origin and means that Islam is less important.

New religious movements

Barker (1999) argues that members of new religious movements are 'disproportionately white'. She does note, however, the exceptions of the Branch Davidians (Waco) and the People's Temple (Jonestown), where members were predominantly working-class blacks.

The People's Temple

Founded in 1953, this cult became based on the Caribbean coast of Guyana in South America. It was the site of the first known mass suicide of modern times. In 1978, 918 people died. Subsequent investigations suggested that at least some deaths were not suicides. The cult was led by Jim Jones, a white man whose leadership style was charismatic. His

Victims of the suicide pact in the Jonestown massacre, Guyana, where over 900 people died

promise to his followers had been a world based on class and racial equality in the eyes of Jesus Christ — an appealing message to poor blacks. (70% of cult members were black.) The isolated location allowed for a largely unchallenged Christian socialist Utopian community to develop. Carrot-and-stick methods were used to keep followers loyal — the carrot being the love and personal relationship with Jones. The stick was a set of relatively severe methods of control, viewed from outside as 'manipulation, physical abuse and brainwashing' (Hall 2003). The mass suicide resulted from increasing pressure and criticism from the American government and media. Hall states that: 'Jim Jones told the assembled residents of Jonestown that they would no longer be able to survive as a community. With a tape recorder running, Jones argued, "If we can't live in peace, then let's die in peace"'.

Hall explains the success of the People's Temple in terms of the lack of racial integration and equality in the USA. Had America been a fairer society, Jones would not have been able to persuade people to follow him. The same could be said of the Branch Davidians (see Chapter 5).

Summary

Social characteristics play an important part in determining the religiosity of a person or group:

- **Social class** In Britain, the middle class seem to be more religious than the working class. This generalisation is not so easy to uphold on a global basis.
- **Gender** On a global basis, whatever type of religion is considered, women appear to be more religious than men. However, men are almost always in charge of religion and the interpretation of its theology.
- **Age** The older people are, the more likely they are to be religious. In general, there is a concern that a lack of religiosity among young people will lead to a breakdown of morality. However, concern is also a expressed when young people, especially Muslims, are too religious.
- **Ethnicity** Ethnic minorities tend to be more religious than the indigenous majority. Their religiosity may reflect that of the host culture, as later generations become more accepted and more settled.

Task 6.8

Outline and discuss the view that a person's social characteristics tell us a good deal about their religiosity.

Guidance

This is structured like a typical OCR question and requires a range of skills to answer it well. You need to:

- show breadth of knowledge and understanding by referring to the arguments that a person's social characteristics — such as class, gender, age and ethnicity — affect their religiosity
- build in evaluation by looking at the strengths and weaknesses of the arguments related to these characteristics.
- plan the whole essay before you begin writing so that you can interweave knowledge and evaluation points throughout

In order to write the essay within the time allowed you could *either* focus on a couple of characteristics in detail *or* summarise the four key characteristics. You should aim to explain a range of studies for the characteristics you cover. Those covered should also be evaluated and compared. What are the similarities between the studies?

The conclusion should explain how sociologists can generalise about people's religiosity if they know something about their social characteristics. It might also consider the implications for the future of religion. Is religion being passed on to younger generations, and how far is this influenced by class, gender and ethnicity? Are Bruce (2002) and Voas (2005) right to be sceptical about the future of religion?

Research suggestion

This area lends itself to questionnaire or interview research on any of the key themes of social class, gender, age and ethnicity. If you can gain access to groups of Christians, non-Christians and people who are not religious, you could ask a range of questions about their religiosity (or lack of it). You could then examine the data to see if there are similarities or contrasts that indicate trends about possible secularisation or increased religiosity and spirituality.

Useful websites

- www.bbc.co.uk/religion/religions/christianity/subdivisions/pentecostal_1.shtml
  This site contains an introduction to Pentecostalism, including links to a video clip, which should help you to understand the nature of black Christianity.
- www.bbc.co.uk/religion/religions/islam/
  This BBC site gives a full introduction to Islam. It covers its beliefs, practices, views on moral issues and aspects of Islamic lifestyle.

Further reading

- Pryce, K. (1979) *Endless Pressure*, Penguin.
  Although dated, this book provides an insight into the workings of the black community in the St Paul's district of Bristol during the late 1970s.
- Modood, T. et al. (1997) 'Changing Ethnic Identities in Britain', in A. Giddens, *Sociology: Introductory Readings*, Polity.
  This extract provides concluding comments and findings on the nature of ethnic-minority religion and its relationship with family, marriage and inclusion in British society.

Glossary

7/7
terrorist attacks on London in 2005

9/11
terrorist attacks on New York and Washington in 2001

adherents
people who follow the rules and beliefs of a religion

agent of secondary socialisation
an institution, outside the immediate family, that teaches culture

Alpha
a Christian movement aimed at introducing people to the word of God in less formal circumstances than in church

Anglican
another word for the Church of England and other churches that share its teachings and structure

Archbishop of Canterbury
spiritual leader of the Church of England

atheism
a belief that there is no such thing as God

believing without belonging
not attending church regularly but being privately committed to religious thinking

burqa
a whole-body covering worn by some Muslim women

capitalism
an economic system based on money and the profit motive

caste
a social hierarchy in Indian society based on inherited divisions between people

charisma
a persuasive and motivating personality

Church
a large-scale, national or international religious organisation

civil religion
nation states acting inclusively to create social solidarity and a collective consciousness

class-consciousness
in a Marxist context, the working class being aware of exploitation and their belief that they could defeat the ruling class through revolution

clergy
officials of a church, for example priests and ministers

collective consciousness
a collective way of thinking, based on sharing the same norms and values

collective worship
a government policy on the requirement of daily gatherings in schools to at least consider moral issues and, ideally, to pray together

colonialism
policy of a country intending to gain power over other countries

colonisation
the rule of one country by another

concepts
key ideas; used in sociology to explain the social world

conflict theory
a theory, such as Marxism or feminism, that emphasises unequal and potentially conflicting relationships

congregation
the 'audience' attending a religious ceremony or service

consensus
agreement

crucify
to kill by hanging from a cross

cult
smaller than a sect; a group making fewer demands on people, who can drift in and out of membership

Darwinians

academics who follow Darwin's views of evolution

denomination

middle tier of religious organisation, willing to compromise with other religions and with the secular world

Dianetics®

central theme of the Church of Scientology; a system designed to remove unwanted images from the mind

diocese

area under the authority of a bishop

divine right of kings

a belief that the king was chosen by God and should be obeyed without question; to challenge the king was to challenge God

ecumenism

a joining together of religions to spread their general message, while ignoring their differences

Emerging Church movement

a Christian movement aimed at introducing people to the Word of God in less formal circumstances than church

established sects

sects that have maintained their size over a number of generations

ethnocentric

viewing one's own culture as better than those of others

European exceptionalism

the argument that, although secularisation may be occurring in institutionalised religion in Europe, this is globally the exception, rather than the rule

evangelists or evangelicals

Christians who follow Christ's words to the disciples to go out and spread the word of God

evolution

slow change based on gradual adaptation to new circumstances

false class-consciousness

according to Marxist beliefs, this is a condition in the minds of working-class people whereby they feel that their position at the bottom of society is fair and appropriate; as a result, they do not feel exploited and, therefore, will not rise up against the ruling class

fissiparousness
a tendency towards splits or schisms

formal religion
a religion based around religious institutions

functional definition
defines religion by reference to what it does, not by what people believe

fundamentalism
belief of fundamentalists that their Holy Book is the word of God and should be adhered to, without question or deviation

golden age of religion
the time when religiosity was at its peak

hegemony
ideological domination, usually by the ruling class

hidden curriculum
issues taught covertly in school

historical materialism
a description of the past, present and future of human relationships in terms of observable 'facts', rather than ideas that are abstract and not probable

ideal type
theoretical outline of an idealised set of characteristics with the aim of focusing sociological research; evidence would be compared with the idea

ideological control
control of society through the control of ideas; a cheaper and more effective method than control through force

ideological state apparatus
institutions (e.g. religion, media and education) that help the ruling class maintain ideological control; they teach the working class that society is fair and cannot be changed

informal religion
private religious worship, without the guidance and leadership of a religious institution

infrastructure

Marx's term for the economic relationships that he thought were the foundation for unequal relationships between people

institution

a structure that people develop to facilitate the organisation of society (e.g. religion, the family and government)

interdependent

working together; functionalists tend to claim that the structures of society need to work together

Koran

the sacred text of Islam

laity

the people, as distinguished from the clergy

lay preacher

in nonconformist churches, an unpaid person who conducts the service in place of the minister

madrassa

an Islamic school

mahram

an escort who poses no sexual threat to a woman, usually a kin member such as a husband, father or older brother

martyr

a person prepared to die for his or her beliefs

Marxist feminists

people who emphasise the role of men in using economic power to oppress women

millenarian or millennial movements

movements that focus their beliefs and activities on the second coming of Christ and/or the creation of heaven on Earth

misogyny

hatred of women

monarch

king or queen; the sole inherited head of state

neo-Durkheimians

sociologists who think that Durkheim was broadly correct, but who would change the emphasis of some elements of his theory

neo-Marxists

sociologists who think that Marx was broadly correct, but who would change the emphasis of some elements of his theory

New Age religion

individualistic religion that lacks formal structure

new religious movements

sects; some are not 'new' and some claim not to be 'religious'

nonconformist

Protestants who are not members of the Anglican Church; originally against the monarch being head of the religion

objectivity

a view based on neutral evidence, rather than on personal bias

operationalisation of concepts

the clear definition of concepts to allow for their effective measurement

organic analogy

a theory that says that society works in a similar way to the human body

paradigm

a conceptual framework within which theories are constructed

parish

a district under the authority of a priest or vicar

patriarchy

a system of male domination

Pentecostalists

Evangelical Christians who believe, among other things, that good Christians are able to speak 'in tongues'

phenomenologists

sociologists who focus on the conscious actions of individuals

Pope

leader of the Roman Catholic Church, based in the Vatican City, Rome

postmodernist
> a sociologist who believes that there can be no single theory of society and the way it works because everyone has individual insight

profane
> not sacred

Protestant ethic
> hard work and a simple life bringing adherents closer to God

Protestantism
> a form of Christianity that grew out of criticisms of the Roman Catholic Church, which was accused of failing to live as Christ had

psychotherapy
> a psychological counselling technique derived from the work of Sigmund Freud

radical feminist
> a person who takes the view that men use physical strength to maintain control over women

relative deprivation
> feeling that one is badly off in comparison with others

reliability
> consistency of results obtained because the observers use the same clear tools for measurement

religiosity
> religious behaviours, including religious thinking and practices

religious institutions
> churches, temples, synagogues and mosques, for example

religious pluralism
> where many variations of religion take over from one church that had a monopoly (as happened in the Reformation)

religious practice
> attendance at religious ceremonies such as regular services, naming ceremonies, marriages and funerals

religious thinking
> beliefs consistent with religious teaching

rites or rituals

religious ceremonies

sacred

something considered holy and beyond ordinary experience

salvation anxiety

a term used by Weber meaning a state of stress for Calvanist Protestants about whether heaven or hell awaited them

schisms

splits or breaks — for example, people leaving a church and forming another

sect

a relatively small religious movement with committed members

secular

not religious

secularisation

the process of religion becoming less important in society

secularist

a person who proposes that religion does not, and should not, enter into the social world

Sharia law

a body of rules from Islamic sacred texts, which guides the lives of Muslims

social significance

the importance of a phenomenon, in this case religion, to society

social solidarity

a feeling of togetherness that makes a group and its members feel psychologically stronger

spirit of capitalism

psychological impetus to ensure that individuals who were motivated by enterprise, collectively created industrial capitalism

spirituality

religious or moral thinking

structural determinism

the view that human behaviour results from the influences of structures, rather than from human consciousness

subjectivity

personal bias as opposed to views based on scientifically collected evidence

substantive definition

a major dimension of religion is belief in a god/gods or another super-empirical being

super-empirical

beyond human measurement

superstructure

Marx's term for the institutions in society that were built upon the economy and that supported unequal economic relationships

theologians

academics who study the messages in holy books, sermons etc.

totemism

a religion that designates a specific object, such as a rock or tree, as 'sacred'

transcendent

beyond human experience

typology

a theoretical outline of central characteristics

universal

found in all societies and in all historical periods

vicariousness

Davie's description of people expecting the minority (clergy and churchgoers) to act on their behalf